QUEEN UNCOVERED

QUEEN UNCOVERED

UNSEEN PHOTOGRAPHS, RARITIES AND INSIGHTS
FROM LIFE WITH A ROCK 'N' ROLL BAND

PETER HINCE

WELBECK

PREFACE

This photography book is not a definitive collection or chronological account of Queen's photographic history – because, simply, I don't have that. No photographer does.

What I am fortunate enough to have is a unique photographic record and the accompanying experiences of living the rock 'n' roll life in the 1970s and 1980s. For eleven years, I worked alongside one of the greatest rock bands the world has ever seen as a roadie and head of their crew. I was never Queen's 'official photographer'. But photography, always a keen interest, grew into a passion and is the career I pursued after leaving Queen, following their final Magic tour in 1986.

During those glory years with Queen I was in an unrivalled, privileged position. Because the band trusted me, I captured images nobody else has. You might say I was lucky but I've found in life that the harder you work, the more you apply yourself and recognise and take opportunities, the luckier you get.

Here I share my journey of those special times via photographs of Queen and associated images of the era. Along with a variety of memorabilia and ephemera, it presents a visual package of life with Queen. I've uncovered many previously unseen and unpublished images and items from my archive, as well as variations on images that may be familiar.

I hope you enjoy my journey.

Peter Hince
London, 2023

INTRODUCTION

The publication of this book coincides with the 50th anniversary of my meeting Queen for the first time, in November 1973.

I was working as a roadie for Mott The Hoople and Ground Control, a sound system and equipment rental company set up by Robin Mayhew, David Bowie's sound engineer, after David had 'retired' Ziggy Stardust just a few months earlier.

1973 is considered by many historians as the defining year of the late 20th century. Britain joined the common market, the EU – which we have now 'Brexited'. The nation was a grey and grim place with trade union upheavals, strikes, power cuts, massive inflation and an oil crisis – not so dissimilar to 2023 as I write.

I was 18 years old and 1973 was certainly one of the defining years of my life. Britain had a 'Cod War' threatening our national dish of fish and chips, McDonald's had yet to reach our shores and a Berni Inn was considered fine dining.

However, when you are young, naïve and invincible these issues mean little. When choosing the best flared trousers, tie-dye T shirt and listening to the finest rock music of the day was all that mattered, the latest cool album conspicuously tucked under your arm when sauntering down the street.

1973 was awash with glam rock. Mott The Hoople were considered a glam rock band, but it was a title they'd been given by others; Mott were simply a great live rock 'n' roll band, who wore a bit more sparkle and glitz to get their music heard. Upon hearing Mott were on the verge of breaking up, David Bowie wrote their biggest hit, 'All The Young Dudes', specifically for them. He loved the band and this munificent gesture kept Mott going and brought them the recognition and success they deserved.

The music business is often portrayed as one in which shady, underhand characters prey on bands purely for financial gain, not for the love of music. And it's absolutely true. Queen has had a history of problems with management and business deals, as is well documented. But there were decent people, like Bowie and others you will soon meet, who would share their talent and success.

MOTT TOUR
STAGE PASS

MOTT the HOOPLE

GROUND CONTROL

I'M WITH DAVID BOWIE AREN'T YOU?

MOTT THE HOOPLE U.K. TOUR '73.

DATE: Monday 12th November.
VENUE: Town Hall,
                 Leeds.

TEL: 0532-20294
MANAGER: Mr.Bragg.
SOUND CHECK-MOTT: 4-00p.m.
DOORS OPEN: 7-00p.m.
QUEEN: 7-30p.m. - 8-05p.m.
MOTT THE HOOPLE: 8-30p.m. - 10-00p.m.

HOTEL: The Post House,
                 Bramhope,
                 Nr. Leeds.
TEL: 097-335-2911.

WANTED
MOTT the HOOPLE
QUEEN

MEL BUSH PRESENTS
NOV. 12 Leeds Town Hall
NOV. 13 Blackburn King George's Hall
NOV. 15 Worcester Gaumont
NOV. 16 Lancaster University
NOV. 17 Liverpool Stadium
NOV. 18 Hanley Victoria
NOV. 19 Wolverhampton Civic
NOV. 20 Oxford New Theatre
NOV. 21 Preston Guildhall
NOV. 22 Newcastle City Hall

NOV. 23 Glasgow Apollo
NOV. 25 Edinburgh Caley Cinema
NOV. 26 Manchester Opera House
NOV. 27 Birmingham Town Hall
NOV. 28 Swansea Brangwyn Hall
NOV. 29 Bristol Colston Hall
NOV. 30 Bournemouth Winter Gardens
DEC. 1 Southend Kursaal
DEC. 2 Chatham Central Hall
DEC. 14 Hammersmith Odeon

REWARD
75mins of the best Rock & Roll music in the land

MOTT ON TOUR
with supporting act
Queen

NOVEMBER
12 Leeds, Town Hall
13 Blackburn, St. George's Hall
15 Worcester, Gaumont
16 Lancaster University
17 Liverpool, Stadium
18 Hanley, Victoria Hall
19 Wolverhampton, Civic Hall
20 Oxford, New Theatre
21 Preston, Guild Hall
22 Newcastle, City Hall

23 Glasgow, Apollo Theatre
25 Edinburgh, Caley Cinema
26 Manchester, Opera House
27 Birmingham, Town Hall
28 Swansea, Brangwyn Hall
29 Bristol, Colston Hall
30 Bournemouth, Winter Gardens
DECEMBER
1 Southend, Kursaal
2 Chatham, Central Hall
14 London, Odeon, Hammersmith

Watch out for Motts new single released early November 'Roll Away The Stone'

Rehearsals for Mott's '73 UK tour were held at Manticore in Fulham, South West London. A former ABC Regal cinema, the facility was owned and run by supergroup Emerson, Lake and Palmer as a production and rehearsal space, and also where 'ELP' stored their vast array of equipment.

The former cinema seats had been ripped out to give sloping access to a proscenium stage, big enough to host the major touring bands of the day: David Bowie, Led Zeppelin, Lou Reed, Jethro Tull, Paul McCartney and Wings, Roxy Music. They all used Manticore.

But despite its illustrious clients, Manticore was not at all glamorous. It was shabby, dim and dank, with no heating. Military surplus parachute silks were draped from the balcony to hold in any warmth supplied by huge gas blower heaters. Solace from the cold came for the bands only when the stage lighting rig was fired up.

Across the road from Manticore was The Golden Lion pub, where all manner of rock stars would gather to chat, drink and sometimes jam. The pub had a tiny stage for live bands – and strippers at lunchtime. There were no minders or security and you could find yourself quite literally hanging out with your favourite guitarists in the gents toilet.

Backstage passes were a rare item. Normally, having scruffy long hair, keys hanging from a clip on your belt and the phrase 'I'm with the band' would suffice. Although, for the Mott '73 tour, promoter Mel Bush utilised a Dymo label maker and plastic clip-on badges, the type used by delegates at conferences for double-glazing salesmen. It was a very different era, with no health and safety, no contracts or terms of employment. Cash was king and the taxman was to be avoided. But then, money was secondary. It was the adventure and excitement of touring, the new places and experiences that attracted young men to a life on the road.

But, as people sometimes ask, what exactly is a roadie?

The term 'roadie' comes from road manager, when bands essentially had just one guy to help them out with the equipment and drive the van. The role evolved when working directly for a band or its individual members; you become a kind of technical valet to musicians. Aside from the dirty, heavy, physical work of shifting equipment, loading trucks and crawling around confined spaces there are the highly specialised skills required to take care of instruments and equipment. Setting up, testing, tuning, repairing and maintaining, in often inclement circumstances.

On top of that, you prepare drinks for your 'master', lay towels out to dab their perspiring brows and light their cigarettes. You pamper them and are always prepared to anticipate what they might want. So a roadie is a combination of Jeeves, a hod carrier, electronics whizz, whipping boy, therapist and mind reader. In time, I was to Fred what Baldrick was to Blackadder, the Admirable Crichton of rock 'n' roll, but without the dress code. John Deacon was somewhat easier...

But the day I first encountered Queen began as any other at rehearsal at Manticore. Mott were a visceral rock band and, off stage, down to earth 'blokes'. To rehearse they wore 'day clothes' – jeans, thick coats, hats and scarves to combat the November cold.

And then Queen arrived.

Contracted to be the support band on the tour, nobody had heard of them. Yet they waltzed in sporting big hair, silks, satins, embroidered ladies' blouses and platform shoes, which in fairness

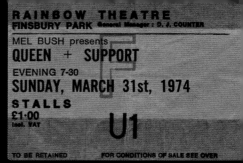

were de rigeur for the time. Even I had a pair with ridiculous heels, totally impractical for working in but worn on days off to look cool.

Queen took to the stage and really went for it, Freddie prancing and posing, whipping up an imaginary audience into a frenzy. They were pushy, somewhat arrogant and knew what they wanted – to go to the very top. Image was seemingly everything, even their sound engineer wore a velvet suit and white gloves to mix their show. Queen certainly had the flair to accompany the flared trousers.

In one of those strange coincidences of life, years after Manticore was demolished it was replaced by what would become my local supermarket. I have worked out that the very spot where I first encountered Freddie Mercury on that day in 1973 is now in the frozen foods aisle, though I'm sure Fred would have preferred it to be in the fine wines and champagne section. I very much doubt he would be happy being associated with own-brand frozen broccoli florets.

At the time, the Mott road crew were somewhat taken aback by the attitude of these 'upstarts'. The general consensus among us was that Queen were a bunch of poseurs and would never make it.

After the end of the '73 Mott tour, culminating with two shows at Hammersmith Odeon, I didn't think Queen would feature in my life again. But less than a year later they were building a loyal following and becoming a headline act, playing at the prestigious Rainbow Theatre in North London. I recall going to see them (free tickets, of course, if you were in the music industry you never paid to see a band) and was amazed at their progression, how polished their act was, especially Freddie's rapport with the audience. They had certainly learned from the experience of touring with Mott and pushed on, finding the next level.

By 1975, the various line-ups of Mott The Hoople and assorted David Bowie and Mick Ronson projects had all but disbanded, so I needed a job. Fortunately, Queen were looking for some new stage crew. And the word was out that they wanted Mott's crew.

Along with Richie and Phil, Mott's two senior roadies, I joined Queen in the summer of 1975 as they recorded the *A Night At The Opera* album, spending my early days with the band flitting between the various studios being used. I picked up an antique harp for Brian May to play on 'Love of My Life', and as we negotiated getting the awkward, delicate instrument down the tricky, narrow access into the Sarm Studios basement, I thought, 'Is this rock 'n' roll? But, hey, it's a job!'. I recall hearing pieces of 'Bohemian Rhapsody' in the various studio control rooms, but not in its entirety until rehearsals at Elstree film studios for the upcoming UK tour. I remember thinking it might be some kind of intro tape for the live show.

The actual intro tapes for the 'NATO' shows were of various classical musical pieces, mostly piano based, which were played softly in the interval, during the changeover from support band Mr Big to Queen. Immediately prior to Queen taking the stage, during a blackout, a tape of an orchestra tuning up was played, at the end of which a conductor taps his baton before announcing, 'Ladies and gentlemen, a night at the opera'.

That tape was recorded and performed by DJ Kenny Everett, a friend and loyal supporter of Queen. He was instrumental in the full six-minute 'Bohemian Rhapsody' being accidentally 'leaked' live on air during his Saturday Capital Radio show. And then 'leaked again, several times in succession. There had been pressure from

management, EMI Records and radio pluggers for Queen to edit the single, until Everett's stunt ensured that Capital's switchboard was jammed with calls about this wonderful new single. No editing ever occurred, Freddie and Queen got their way and the rest is history.

As rehearsals got underway for putting together a new live show, the band would be working virtually 24/7, rehearsing in the day and back in the studio through the night, doing final overdubs, bouncing tracks and mixing. Queen's work ethic was phenomenal and I knew I had to pull my weight if I was to keep up with them – and keep my job.

Which I was very keen to do. After all, I was on £40 a week. Every week! Plus per diem. What more could a 20-year-old want? Stenciling the address of John Reid Enterprises – the company of Queen's new manager, who also managed Elton John – onto equipment flight cases was exciting in itself. And it was not John Reid's Mayfair office, grand enough in its own right, but his office in Beverly Hills, California. Another statement that Queen had arrived in the big time.

Not only did Queen work incredibly hard, they had a high level of professionalism, enthusiasm and drive. Because I was around very talented and focused people it drove me on. Just as well, since working with Fred you had to be at the top of your game, no margin for error. He could be intimidating and demanding, but it simply made me sharper and work harder.

The UK tour was a huge success and, with 'Bohemian Rhapsody' and *A Night At The Opera* both at number one in the charts, gave everybody involved a sense of confidence and swagger. The tour was capped off with another Hammersmith Odeon performance, this time live on BBC Television on Christmas Eve, 1975. A daunting task, as there were very few live broadcast performances by rock bands on TV back then. A nationwide Christmas Eve audience heightened the pressure, as well as satisfying the packed house who had paid to see the band. Giving up Christmas was just one of the many personal sacrifices that had to be made when you work for a rock 'n' roll band.

But Queen rose above their nerves. The show was so well rehearsed and honed from the tour, they took the opportunity to push themselves to yet another level and gave a fantastic performance, possibly one of their best ever.

The new year brought a Pan American 747 flight to New York (in the smoking section, of course) and a major US headline tour, followed by a break in Hawaii en route to sell-out shows in Japan. The tour finished in Australia, playing all the major cities. Queen really were the band of the moment, and at the start of a journey that I would be on for the next decade. It was simply wonderful, and I felt privileged to be a part of it.

The adventure that started fifty years ago is now enjoying a golden anniversary, one of golden memories. I hope you enjoy them.

```
Cont/...... 5   QUEEN TOUR

DATE                 Saturday 29th November - 2nd December
DEPARTURE FROM       London
DEPARTURE TIME
VENUE                Odeon Theatre,
                     Queen Caroline St., HAMMERSMITH
MANAGER              Mr. Phil Leivers
Tel No.              01 748 8660
Back Stage           01 748 2688
EQUIPMENT ARRIVAL    10.00 a.m.
DOORS OPEN           7.00 p.m.
SHOW COMMENCES       7.30 p.m.

HOTELS               QUEEN                      ROAD CREW
                     London                     London

                     * * * * * * * *

DATE                 Wednesday 3rd December - DAY OFF
                                 (possibly Hammersmith Odeon)

                     * * * * * * * *

DATE                 Thursday 4th December - DAY OFF
                                 (possibly Hammersmith Odeon)

                     * * * * * * * *

DATE                 Friday 5th December - DAY OFF - London

                     * * * * * * * *

DATE                 Saturday 6th December - DAY OFF

                     QUEEN                      ROAD CREW
                     London                     The Post House,
                                                Chapel Lane,
                                                Great Barr, Birmingham
                                                Tel 021 357 7444

                     * * * * * * * *
```

Assorted items including a copy of *A Night at the Opera* signed by the band for my mum, after the first show at the Birmingham Odeon; an item she treasures. I don't actually have a set of Queen's autographs – it was not the done thing to ask. It's effectively asking your boss. Would a solicitor ask one of the firm's partners for an autograph? Maybe on a cheque...

CHAPTER 1

SUMMER OF '76

The long, hot summer of 1976 in Britain has become a point of reference in our history when, pre-climate change, there were proper summers.

Having recently finished the Night At The Opera world tour, Queen took a short break before coming back to work on a new album. The band's original plan had been to base themselves at a large villa in Portugal, using The Rolling Stones' mobile recording truck. 'Yeah,' I thought, 'I can put up with that...'

However, the band wanted to be closer to their families after spending long periods of time away touring, so Portugal became England. The process started with rehearsals at Ridge Farm in the leafy county of Surrey, where Queen had rehearsed prior to recording A Night At The Opera. Familiarity breeds success, perhaps?

At Ridge Farm we stayed onsite in various rooms and cottages, working, eating and socialising together for several weeks. It's where I began to get to know Queen a little better as people. On tour, the crew and band travelled separately and mostly stayed in different hotels, so apart from soundcheck and shows we rarely saw each other – and even then it was purely professional.

At the farm, the only people in residence were Freddie, Brian, Roger, John, their respective wives and girlfriends and a small crew, so the band felt secure. No outsiders meant no need for them to put on a persona for the press or public and the atmosphere was professional, of course, but more relaxed.

The success of NATO had given the band real belief and confidence to go forward, buoyed by the support of manager John Reid, who had given them the platform to create their best music and live shows.

Work was done in the main historic black and white barn. The hours varied, as the barn wasn't air-conditioned and the swimming pool area held more appeal during that hot summer. Rough demos were recorded by John Harris, Queen's original and long-standing sound engineer.

Next stop was another bucolic location: The Manor, Virgin Records boss Richard Branson's country estate and studio in Oxfordshire. It was another residential studio with a somewhat hippy feel, where some staff chanted Buddhist mantras in the attic. A magnificent manor house with a studio annex is where we worked and sometimes played. I recall that 'Somebody to Love' was the first track worked on, with 'Tie Your Mother Down' another early song put down on 24-track tape.

Playtime was in a TV lounge where that summer's Olympic Games in Montreal were a popular watch, on one of the three channels available in 1976. There was also a snooker room with a full-sized table, which Fred enjoyed playing. I remember him playing while listening to The Beatles' 'White Album' one day, when he enthused dramatically, 'Just listen to those chords!' Although Queen's music was sometimes quirky, eclectic and different, they held great respect for their musical peers and elders. They were no doubt influenced to some degree by bands such as The Beatles, The Stones, The Who, Led Zeppelin – and Jimi Hendrix was virtually idolized, particularly by Fred.

At this time Queen had finally got some real money and set about buying homes and new cars. Roger was the band's 'petrol head' and upgraded his Alfa Romeo sports car to a shiny black Range Rover, complete with sunroof. One day, proud to show off his new purchase, he set off over the grounds of The Manor, claiming that the 4 wheel drive vehicle could go anywhere. Not long later, he got stuck not far from the house – and The Manor's technical engineer had to pull the Range Rover free with an old army truck.

I didn't have a flash new motor, just the John Reid office VW van, which was deemed 'not appropriate' when I offered to drive Fred back to London later that night to see Mary Austin, his girlfriend, who was unwell. The Manor offered one of their vehicles instead, a Ford estate. Setting off in the dead of night for London I felt the brakes on the car were a little 'spongy' but didn't

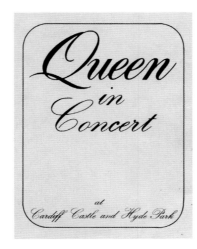

mention it to Fred as he'd have no idea what that meant, having never driven himself – something he maintained his entire life.

As we approached London on the A40 there were a series of roundabouts and road works. I changed down a gear as I approached a roundabout and pressed the brake pedal. Nothing happened. Pumping the brake pedal furiously, I fought to steer the car around to the exit, but lost control and crashed into a pile of drainpipes on the roadside. A headline flashed into my mind: 'Roadie Kills Rock Star!'

As we came to an abrupt halt, I shot a look over to Fred and he back to me. We nodded that we were okay before we even spoke. Not a scratch or bruise. Catching our breath, we were interrupted by a knock on the window and the somewhat alarming sight of faces pressing up against it.

They were Travellers (Gypsies, we knew them as back then) who often parked their caravans along this stretch of the A40 and were concerned about us. We thanked them and confirmed all was well. The Travellers suggested that if we were drunk or had stolen the car it was better to leave soon, before the police showed up. I was stone cold sober and the car was off the road, so what next? Fred took control – he would go for help! For someone who spent the majority of his life having people do things for him, Fred could be very resourceful when needed, a trait that was very evident in his professional life too.

Freddie Mercury, the elusive, stylish Queen megastar was in faded blue jeans, white clogs and an embroidered black silk kimono a Japanese fan had given him. He'd not shaved for a couple of days and his carefully tousled hair was rather ruffled as he wandered off towards some lights in the distance to try to call Mary and his London driver, Derek. As I waited, a passing motorist stopped, enquiring as to my welfare, then kindly offered to call a tow truck

for the wrecked car. There were no mobile phones back then, he'd do it from the next red call box he could find.

When Fred returned, giggling, he told me of the situation comedy that had unfolded. Knocking on the door of the first house he came to, he was quickly recognised. The surprised inhabitants let him use the phone and offered him tea. He graciously accepted but had no money to repay their kindness (he never carried cash). The electricity meter ran out, so they had to go next door to borrow some 10p pieces to feed the meter and boil the kettle – but then discovered that there was no milk for the tea, so another dash next door was needed! Next door also immediately recognised Fred and came round to join the tea party.

On his return, Fred reassured me he had eventually called The Manor and somebody was coming to pick me up. Shortly, Derek arrived at the scene in Fred's Mercedes, and I was still suffering from shock as he took off for London. A tow truck duly arrived and the wrecked car was taken away.

As the wagon train of vehicles arrived from The Manor all they found was me sitting on my briefcase, chain smoking. Somewhat puzzled, Roger asked me what had happened as Fred had relayed the accident, in his usual dramatic fashion, as hideous carnage and the twisted, charred remains of a vehicle. Roger kindly took me to his house and gave me a few stiff drinks.

"No outsiders meant no need for them to put on a persona for the press or public and the atmosphere was professional, of course, but more relaxed."

Scenes of rest and relaxation at Ridge Farm. Left: A big lover of nature, Brian would wander the lush grounds of the farm.

Top: The white grand piano that Fred was in love with for a time, used on 'Bohemian Rhapsody' and in London Queen shows in '75 and '76. It was rented from Chapel Music.

Rehearsing in the converted black and white barn at Ridge Farm. The view from the balcony shows how much equipment was crammed in. We managed to make enough space to get around the pool table, however.

Above: Fred's birthday at The Manor. Studio staff looking at Polaroids taken by Fred with his state of the art SX-70 camera. During live shows he would occasionally take Polaroids of the audience and then throw them into the crowd.

Right: Recording with studio engineer Mike Stone. Mike had worked on all previous Queen albums,and was renowned for his techniques in creating their multi-tracked, three-part vocal harmonies. After his important input as assistant producer on *News Of The World* Mike went on to work more in the USA, having huge success producing Journey, Asia and Whitesnake, among others.

Roger's go-anywhere four-wheel drive Range Rover gets stuck and needs to be towed out. In the background, Fred looks on in a silk kimono.

METROPOLITAN POLICE

Mr Peter Raymond HINCE
8 Malbrook Road
Putney
S.W.15

....Southall..............
..........Police... Station
....67. High. Street......
....SOUTHALL..............
....Middlesex.............
....12th. August,19.76..

Your Ref............................ Our Ref. ....XG.7371...............

Subject:

Sir,

I am directed by the Commissioner of Police of the
Metropolis to refer to the incident which occurred
on 1st August, 1976, at Western Avenue, Northolt,
junction with Ealing Road, arising out of the use
of motor vehicle, index number KYL 157 K and to say
that, after careful consideration, Police have
decided not to take any further action in this
matter.

                   I am, Sir,
                   Your obedient Servant,

                   Chief Inspector (Admin)
               for Chief Superintendent

No. 144A

YOUR OBEDIENT SERVANT

Shortly after the Ford estate incident with Fred I had to present myself and my documentation to a police station, as it was alleged I was driving too fast as I approached the roundabout. Well, any speed is too fast if there are no brakes! Inspections showed the car's brakes were faulty, and the police took no action against me.

Some time later, a music press interview offered Fred dramatic opportunity to relate how the incident had affected him. He replied that his life had flashed before his eyes – and he had wondered who would look after his cats. 'And the roadie actually screamed!'

Fred did commend me for getting so far around the roundabout before we crashed and never held me responsible in any way. I'm happy to say I drove him many times after that – even in an old Ford Transit van!

This page: September saw Queen play shows in Cardiff (top, at Cardiff Castle), Edinburgh (above) and Hyde Park. The Edinburgh Playhouse, built on a hill, was not designed for big rock 'n' roll shows. All the equipment had to be hoisted in a net by crane onto a scaffold tower platform and then wheeled through a hole in the backstage wall. A roadie's nightmare!

Opposite and overleaf: The Hyde Park show utilised the famous orange stage used by The Rolling Stones at Knebworth just a few weeks earlier. In the production office at Hyde Park, legendary tour manager Gerry Stickells sits with a model of the tent and plans for show set-up. The crew were given framed award plaques as a thank you for the show.

QUEEN

A very big thank you

JOHN DEACON   **BRIAN MAY**

FREDDIE MERCURY   **ROGER TAYLOR**

Presented to
Peter Hince
Hyde Park Summer Rock Festival
18th. September 1976

QUEEN

CHAPTER 2
ON THE ROAD

Touring is the lifeblood of rock bands. Back in the 1970s and 1980s it was done primarily to promote and establish a band and boost sales of their records, seven- and twelve-inch-diameter discs of black vinyl that are surprisingly, in this digital age of instant gratification, back in fashion.

Touring is a direct, tangible method to break new markets, sustain the major ones and – along with radio, TV and the press – ensure nobody had forgotten who you were when a new album was released.

There is a certain magic to seeing a live band. It's a there and then, in the moment experience. It's rock 'n' roll kudos to claim, 'I saw Queen at Wembley', 'Led Zeppelin at Earls Court', 'Bowie at Hammersmith Odeon' or 'The Stones in Hyde Park'. It was all live. There was no YouTube or streaming and in the 1970s video recorders were very expensive and not mainstream. They were also the size of a small bungalow and needed a couple of roadies to carry one.

A touring rock 'n' roll show is akin to a circus, a temporary travelling residency featuring similar characters: clowns, high wire acts, a ringmaster, daredevils, animal trainers with dangerous wild beasts! And of course, the stars of the show.

Every tour starts with rehearsals. Whether it's a brand-new tour to promote a freshly released album or a different leg of a world tour, the set needs to be reviewed and refreshed, the lighting and stage set worked on and a plan made for how to incorporate the new songs and elements of the show. Sometimes we were lucky enough to be able to rehearse in the same venue that the tour started, avoiding the upheaval and cost of moving the entire production and personnel.

Once on the road, touring relies emphatically on communication, primarily between the band and their audience and then the complex combinations of communication between the band and crew, tour manager, stage manager, promoter, production manager, union officials, truck drivers and border officials. Trillions of human neural synapses. Remarkably, all of this was achieved before the arrival of the internet.

Sat nav? We used things called maps, that folded out to view where you were and where you planned to go. Handy books known as 'The A–Z' of various cities were also utilised. But it was experience, improvisation and diligence that actually got us from Amsterdam to Zagreb, Aachen to Zurich, Arizona to... somewhere in the USA beginning with 'z'.

We all have to handle situations with the tools available to us at the time. If, in 1975, somebody had told me about a smartphone and what could be achieved with it, I'd ask if they'd been watching *Star Trek* or smoked too much weed. Possibly both.

Touring builds camaraderie, character and a sense of purpose. Despite working closely with a large group of people, the relationships forged and banter exchanged, touring could actually become a somewhat solitary existence. I was always at the beck and call of what Queen did and wanted, so could never really plan for a holiday. I sometimes didn't see my parents or family for a year at a time, except when they came to a live show in England.

Touring personnel need to bond quickly, to set their territory and guard it. Everything is intensified on tour, you grow up quickly or fall by the wayside. It was tough, both physically and mentally. The process of touring and the purported glamour associated with a transient, on the road lifestyle has some truth to it. But the reality is somewhat less romantic.

While the band and their entourage are snuggled up in Egyptian cotton sheets and five-star comfort, the crew are scraping themselves out of an unlaundered bunk after little sleep to a day of physical and mental labour, with no health and safety to speak of.

To be fair to Queen, they had enormous pressure on them 24/7. When the crew's initial job of preparing everything was done it was then up to the band to perform a show to the highest level, albeit assisted by the crew. But once those truck doors closed, we were free until they opened at the next venue, whereas the band had to continually perform, to the press, waiting fans, record companies, radio stations, TV interviews and on and on...

With Queen we travelled the world. America was the dream, the promised land and where the money and fame was. Rock 'n' roll's high table.

Back in 1976, you not only needed a visa to enter the USA, but a smallpox vaccination certificate and a signed, declared entry form that you were not and never had been a member of the Communist Party. Or had been on a farm recently.

In the '70s and '80s, this was the lucrative market where rock bands could establish themselves as being 'big'. And America was all about big: big bucks, tour venues, billboards, cars, highways, attitudes, plates of food and big hair that topped plus-size ladies' bottoms. Happy days.

The rooms in American hotels, albeit in chains such as Holiday Inn, Ramada, Sheraton, were much more spacious and comfortable than those that housed the crews in Europe. Proper showers, not an attachment on the bath taps, with good water pressure. Countless TV channels on the colour sets in the shag-pile-carpeted rooms, though surprisingly the colour and picture quality was far inferior to the UK; people's faces tended to be either magenta or green and fuzzy, as if in a horror B-movie.

America was geared up for touring rock bands, with its easily accessible arenas, convention centres, sports venues and coliseums. Life on tour was generally more comfortable for road crew than in Europe at the time. Customised buses with bunks, air conditioning, ice boxes, TV, sound systems, shag-pile carpet that gave static shocks – and a WC. Despite these comforts, living for weeks on end with eleven other men who had differing levels of personal hygiene, among other unsavoury habits, could become incendiary. Hence the fairly regular purchase of fireworks to let off steam, with loud bangs and fizzing trails of colour into the air – or hotel corridor.

There was always an undercurrent of volatility on tour, one that could spill over into shouting matches and hostility between lighting, sound and band crew, who had quite different personalities as well as nationalities. However, fisticuffs were very rarely involved and an astute tour manager could defuse simmering tensions before they reached this level.

The US venues had experienced, professional union crews who helped unload and load trucks, move the equipment around and assist with technical and physical work. Catering was supplied to sustain us, consisting of mostly meat and broccoli with baked potatoes, garnished with something called sour cream? A noble attempt to give us the English national dish of fish and chips for dinner failed miserably. But it was free...

Tour itineraries were set by booking agents with a sense of hubris but little notion of practical and logistical issues. Some tours were seemingly planned using a map of America, a set of darts and a blindfold.

Touring Europe in the '70s and '80s was an experience as diverse as the countries Queen played in, and tours were generally tougher and more demanding than those in America. Fortunately, we had seasoned truck and bus drivers who did nothing but tour the UK and continental Europe. American crew often found Europe confusing. Different languages, money, cultures, border crossings, work permits, travel, withholding taxes... One of the beauties of Europe was (and still is) that you can travel through three countries in a matter of hours and experience completely different cultures and cuisines.

Queen always pushed the limits with their studio productions and their live shows extended that ethos to the countries they played. In 1979 we crossed the Iron Curtain and played two shows in former Yugoslavia – Zagreb and Ljubljana – now the capitals of Croatia and Slovenia respectively.

Although working conditions in Eastern Europe were not what we were used to, there was an excitement of the unknown, crossing into Soviet territory.

You will find in this chapter that the photographs are more focused on the aspects of life on the road away from the stage show itself – there are relatively few images of the band on stage performing. The reason for this is that I was not Queen's live photographer, I was Freddie and John's roadie and my job was to focus on them during shows, hit the many cues required and be aware at all times of what they might need.

I only ever took photographs of live shows when I was specifically asked. If Fred had caught me with a camera during a show he would not have been happy – quite the opposite in fact!

This photograph was taken during a gruelling tour in early 1977, when Queen first played the really big venues such as New York's Madison Square Garden, the LA Forum, Chicago Stadium, Boston Garden and Cobo Hall in Detroit, as well as Canada's top venues, Maple Leaf Gardens in Toronto and the Montreal Forum.

Queen were managed from 1975 to 1978 by John Reid, who also managed Elton John. We used the same equipment warehouse and same American sound and lighting companies, which is why you can see an Elton flight case in the photo. For this early '77 US tour Elton had loaned Freddie his 9-foot Steinway grand piano so that he could have the same instrument for every show. Previously, Fred had to play whatever grand piano was supplied by the local promoter, which varied in sound and touch. For the late '77 US tour Freddie selected, from three supplied at rehearsals, a 9-foot Steinway D, American model. This remained his stage piano for the rest of his career with Queen. It was even transported to Montreux in '78 and used on the *Jazz* album, notably on the hit 'Don't Stop Me Now'.

Top right: On tour everybody was allocated luggage tags with a number, which would correspond with your name and on hotel room lists. In principle a good idea, but Queen luggage tags were attractive items and often went 'missing', especially when flying. This set for the early '77 US tour includes my number on my stage pass too – in case I forgot who I was.

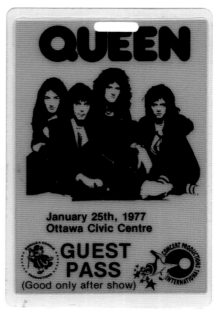

Queen were synonymous with spectacular live shows: innovative stage sets, enormous lighting rigs, pyrotechnics and smoke, which set the stage for the band to perform a set of their music ranging from tender ballads to full-on, smash-your-head rockers. There was a palpable energy on the stage when Queen were really in synch with each other and rocking – the foot would start to tap, the head nod and vicariously the crew could feel part of the performance.

Scenes of life on the road: winding roads, stage sets and concert venues. **Top:** Cobo Arena in Detroit. Always a great venue to play, with a raucous rock 'n' roll crowd. A bitterly cold place in January, it sat alongside the often frozen St. Lawrence River, with Canada on the other side. Here we see the upcoming attractions including rock bands Rush and Kiss, plus the Detroit Pistons Basketball team, the world's greatest gospel show – and wrestling. Something for everybody in 'Motown'. **Above:** The crew pose in front of Elvis Presley's plane, the *Lisa Marie*, in the snowy and icy conditions of Casper, Wyoming during a refuelling stop, en route

LONG BEACH

John Harris, pictured above with Roger Taylor, was Queen's original roadie and sound engineer. He would record every show on cassette from the mixing desk for review by himself or the band. Poignantly, the cassette above is the last show in late '77 before John was tragically struck with a serious illness, which took him several years to recover from.

Right: Crossroads of the World on Sunset Boulevard, Hollywood, California. What an address! It is where Queen's US office was based with tour manager Gerry Stickells' GLS Productions. GLS moved in the mid '80s to a unit on Zoetrope, Francis Ford Coppola's studio complex on North Las Palmas in Hollywood. Again, a rather impressive base. Queen rehearsed on a sound stage here for the 1982 Hot Space tour.

yes, there really is a Kalamazoo

OHIO
70-37
TRUCK STOP
Rte. 1 - Hebron, Ohio 43025

USA 21c
UNITED STATES AIR MAIL
POST CARD

GLS PRODUCTIONS INC.

Rainbow bar & grill

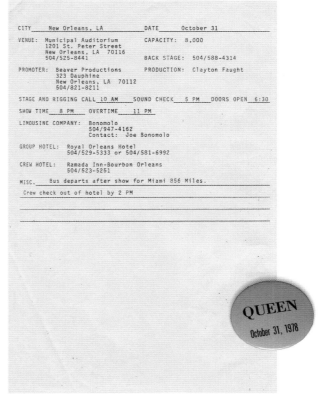

CITY____New Orleans, LA_____DATE_____October 31_____

VENUE: Municipal Auditorium   CAPACITY: 8,000
        1201 St. Peter Street
        New Orleans, LA 70116
        504/525-8441   BACK STAGE: 504/588-4314

PROMOTER: Beaver Productions   PRODUCTION: Clayton Faught
           323 Dauphine
           New Orleans, LA 70112
           504/821-8211

STAGE AND RIGGING CALL_10 AM____SOUND CHECK___5 PM___DOORS OPEN__6:30

SHOW TIME___8 PM____OVERTIME____11 PM_____

LIMOUSINE COMPANY: Bonomolo
                    504/947-4162
                    Contact: Joe Bonomolo

GROUP HOTEL: Royal Orleans Hotel
              504/529-5333 or 504/581-6992

CREW HOTEL: Ramada Inn-Bourbon Orleans
             504/523-5251

MISC.___Bus departs after show for Miami 856 Miles._____

Crew check out of hotel by 2 PM

ALL THAT JAZZ

The 1978 *Jazz* album was launched with a party after the show in the city of jazz, New Orleans. Held on Halloween, the party has entered the annals of rock 'n' roll folklore as being totally wild and debauched. Not untrue. However, the tale of dwarfs mingling among the revellers with bowls of cocaine strapped to their heads is untrue.

We had plenty more parties over the years, notably in New York in 1980, when Queen had sold out three consecutive nights at Madison Square Garden. Upon hearing that the backstage entertainment was to be female mud wrestlers, Fred quipped, 'Well if you guys are having that, then I want gay dwarfs with moustaches in leather shorts to serve the drinks!'

Taking out a notepad, Gerry Stickells responded, 'Sure, this is New York – how many do you want Fred?'

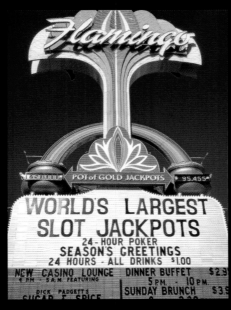

WE WILL ROCK YOU

Following the huge success of their 1980 album *The Game*, Queen toured the globe and broke new territories in 1981 with South America. It was their most successful album, with two number one singles in the US, and during this period Queen became exactly what they had always wanted to be: the biggest band in the world.

The live show was fantastic, honed to perfection, with a balance of new material and classic earlier songs. To capture this it was decided to play and film two near-identical live concerts at the Montreal Forum to make a movie for the cinema. Montreal was always a fun town to visit on tour.

In later years this *We Will Rock You* movie was edited and remastered with superb quality and renamed *Queen Rock Montreal*. The result shows Queen live at their very best.

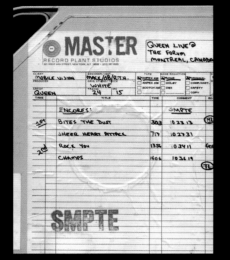

ROCK 'N' ROLL PIANO

Canadian Fred Mandel was brought in to play back-up keyboards for the US and Japan Hot Space tours. An incredibly talented musician and great guy, he also contributed to many songs on *The Works* album as well as working with Brian and Freddie on their solo projects. Here he plays rock 'n' roll piano on Freddie's Steinway for 'Crazy Little Thing Called Love', when he would get his introduction to the audience.

  Once Fred had got to know the band, he cheekily said to Freddie, 'With two Freds on tour it might get confusing. Do you think you could change your name?' Freddie laughed heartily. That sort of humour was rife among Queen and their entourage.

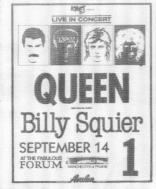

```
CITY:      NEW YORK                    DATE:  Tuesday, 30 September 80

Venue:     MADISON SQUARE GARDEN    Capacity:      19,000
           8 Penn Plaza (Employees Ent)
           33rd Street & 8th Avenue  Backstage:    212-563-8256/8197
           New York, New York 10001

           212-563-8000

Promoter:  ARDEE PRODUCTIONS        Contact:      KEITH KEVAN
           27 East 67th Street
           New York, New York 10021

           212-249-7773

STAGE CALL:  __8:00a__  SOUND CHECK:  __4:00__  DOORS OPEN:  __7:00p__

SHOW TIME:   __8:00p__

QUEEN:

HOTEL:     WALDORF ASTORIA TOWERS  212-355-3000
           301 Park Avenue
           New York, New York 10022

LIMOUSINE:  East Wind    212-247-4400           Contact:  Terry


CREW:

HOTEL:     SOUTHGATE TOWERS  212-563-1800
           31st Street & 7th Avenue
           New York, New York 10001


NOTE:  After the last show equipement load in container.
```

This page: Scenes from the Big Apple show the prestigious Madison Square Garden that Queen revelled in playing. Once you had played to a sold out 'Garden' you were in the big time. An arena holding almost 20,000 people on the fifth floor, you could literally feel the floor move when Queen rocked New York.

Opposite: The call sheet for Queen's final live performance in the USA, an appearance on *Saturday Night Live*. Hosted by Chevy Chase, the show included two live performances by the band.

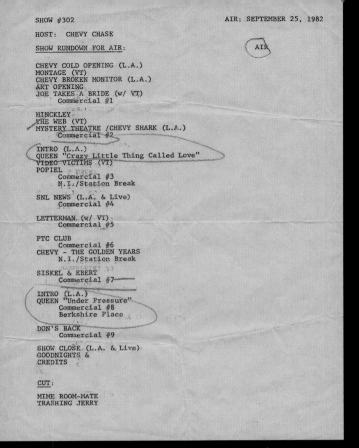

```
SHOW #302                           AIR: SEPTEMBER 25, 1982

HOST:  CHEVY CHASE

SHOW RUNDOWN FOR AIR:                        AIR

CHEVY COLD OPENING (L.A.)
MONTAGE (VT)
CHEVY BROKEN MONITOR (L.A.)
ART OPENING
JOE TAKES A BRIDE (w/ VT)
         Commercial #1

HINCKLEY
THE WEB (VT)
MYSTERY THEATRE /CHEVY SHARK (L.A.)
         Commercial #2

INTRO (L.A.)
QUEEN "Crazy Little Thing Called Love"
VIDEO VICTIMS (VT)
POPIEL
         Commercial #3
         N.I./Station Break

SNL NEWS (L.A. & Live)
         Commercial #4

LETTERMAN (w/ VT)
         Commercial #5

PTC CLUB
         Commercial #6
CHEVY - THE GOLDEN YEARS
         N.I./Station Break

SISKEL & EBERT
         Commercial #7

INTRO (L.A.)
QUEEN "Under Pressure"
         Commercial #8
         Berkshire Place

DON'S BACK
         Commercial #9

SHOW CLOSE (L.A. & Live)
GOODNIGHTS &
CREDITS

CUT:

MIME ROOM-MATE
TRASHING JERRY
```

SATURDAY NIGHT LIVE

Queen's final live performance in the USA took place on September 25th, 1982, in New York City. It was not at Madison Square Garden, which had become a regular venue for the band, but at NBC TV studios in the Rockefeller Centre, to perform on the prestigious *Saturday Night Live* show. The Hot Space tour had finished at The Forum in Los Angeles ten days earlier, all of the equipment loaded into sea containers for the upcoming tour of Japan, with the exception of that required for the SNL recording. This was a live show, no miming to backing tracks. Queen played two slots on the show, performing 'Crazy Little Thing Called Love', their big number one hit of 79–'80, on the first, and 'Under Pressure', from the current *Hot Space* album, during the second.

The warm-up act for the small audience was Eddie Murphy, starting to make a name for himself in America as a regular on *SNL*. Backstage, as I tuned guitars, Eddie paced up and down muttering his lines. 'Hi man', he nodded to me. 'Alright mate', I replied, having no idea who he was at the time.

"A touring rock 'n' roll show is akin to a circus, a temporary travelling residency featuring similar characters."

#242

ROCK YOU
ENTERTAIN YOU
SOMEBODY TO LOVE
BEAT EM JOIN EM

(DEATH ON 2 LEGS
(KILLER QUEEN
) BICYCLE RACE
 LOVE WITH MY CAR
 GET DOWN MAKE LOVE
 BEST FRIEND

NOW IM HERE
DONT STOP ME NOW
SPREAD YOURS

(DREAMERS BALL
 LOVE OF MY LIFE
(39

ITS LATE
BRIGHTON ROCK
FAT BOTTOMED GIRLS
KEEP YOURSELF ALIVE
BO RHAP
TIE YOUR MOTHER
―――――――――――――
① S. HEART ATTACK
② ROCK YOU / CHAMPS

LIFE IS NOT A REHEARSAL

A tour was always preceded by production rehearsals.
For the 1979 European tour, shown here, both rehearsals
and the first show took place at the Ernst Merck Halle in
Hamburg, always a fun place to spend time.
Right is an original set list for the rehearsals, handwritten
by me and then photocopied many times at the Park
Hochhaus Hotel. My room number is written in the corner
so I could be charged for the copies. The set list was
chopped and changed during a tour, often if Fred's voice
was suffering. So notes and amendments were made to the
virgin set list you see here. It was my job to get the agreed
set from Fred before the show and then convey it to the
various members of the crew – sound, monitors, lighting,
stage manager and the drum and guitar roadies too.

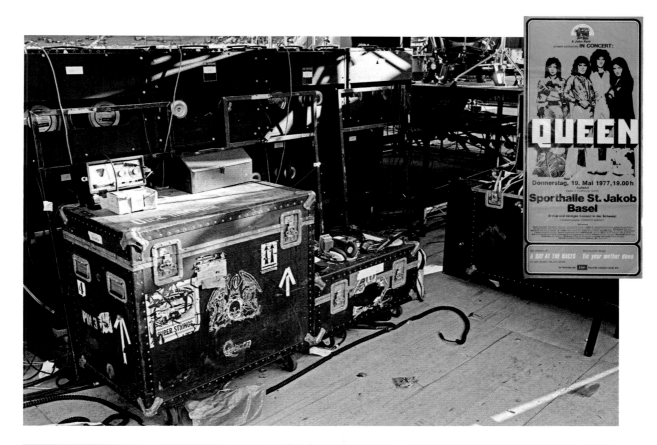

When Queen toured Europe it was the era of the Berlin Wall, the Cold War between west and east. So a trip to Berlin had both a sense of excitement and trepidation. The former German capital still held the hedonism and decadence of its 1930s heyday, and the inhabitants were literally living on the edge – so let's party hard, as tomorrow the Russians might come marching in!

The major venue there could only be played in the summer months. The Waldbuhne – literally 'stage in the wood' – was an amphitheatre surrounded by trees and greenery, in the shadow of the Olympic stadium, both built for the 1936 games. Hitler gave speeches at the Waldbuhne, and the original tunnels where he accessed the stage from were used for equipment access. A somewhat spectacular but eerie place for a show.

Berlin

VER" and join the Party CCCP
OR STAY AND BAT...

Above: Brian sits in the front row, taking in the atmosphere of the Waldbuhne in Berlin.

Below, right: Frankfurt's Festhalle. A concert here in February 1979, provided much of the material for the *Live Killers* double LP.

Opposite: Queen's adventurous spirit took us further afield, to venues in Zagreb and beyond.

Queen Invite you to a Party

to celebrate the end of the Hot Space Tour

Date: 5th June 1982
Venue: Embassy Club
Old Bond Street W.1
Time: 11.45 pm onwards
Dress: Suspenders, shorts or anything unconventional

RSVP: Sara, 46 Pembridge Road, W.11
Telephone: 01-727 5641

ADMIT ONE

Above right: Keyboard player Morgan Fisher, once the keyboard player in Mott The Hoople. He was well known to Queen and became the first additional musician to play live with the band, during the European Hot Space tour.

Opposite: Soundcheck on the Hot Space tour. John played rhythm guitar on 'Staying Power' as the bass parts were covered by Morgan Fisher, before Fred Mandel took over for the US and Japan Hot Space tours.

CHAPTER 3

MUNICH

→20　　　　→20A　　　4　4　5　　→21A

→23　　　　→23A　　　　→24　　　　→24A

During the summer of 1979, Queen arrived in Munich for a six-week stay in order to finish off a complex tax year spent outside of the UK, one which had started in summer 1978 in Montreux.

Munich and Montreux shared two things in common: they began with the letter M and both were home to top recording studios. After that the differences were pronounced, two totally different environments, cultures and attitudes. Montreux: serene, picturesque, somewhat antiseptic and, being a much-policed state, everybody wrapped up for bed with their cocoa by 9pm. The antithesis to Munich, a pulsating, liberal city where anything goes – and did, 24/7, including public holidays and weekends.

After a week of rehearsals on a sound stage in Munich's Pucheim film studios, we moved into Musicland recording studio. Shortly afterwards I flew to London to clear Queen's touring equipment, returning from Japan by sea container, through customs. Before heading back to Munich, the Queen office asked me if I could take 'something' back with me. I was expecting it to be videos of UK television, English sausages, or maybe paperwork to sign.

'It's Freddie,' the secretary told me. 'You'll have to travel with him, in first class.'

'Well, if I have to…'

Freddie had also briefly returned to London, but needed to get back to Munich promptly, as he had no more allocated tax days in the UK left. But we hit a problem in the shape of an air traffic controllers' strike at Heathrow Airport. I immediately went to Heathrow to monitor the increasingly tense situation. Freddie's tax status was becoming a serious concern, he had to leave the UK that day. A carefully planned year of writing, recording and touring overseas would be ruined, potentially costing millions of pounds. Hiring a private aeroplane was not an option, the strike affected their airspace too.

I made enquiries about renting a car; we could drive together to Dover and take a ferry to Europe, just to get Freddie out of the UK, a stamp in his passport. I felt under severe pressure for something that was out of my control. Fortunately, after a few hours, the Munich flight was cleared to depart. I called Freddie at home and he was driven at speed to Heathrow.

On board the British Airways flight we relaxed, enjoying a glass or several of champagne, and chatted about music and how much we both enjoyed Munich and the exciting nightlife. For different reasons.

Having played several shows in Munich, Queen loved the city, its people and liberal atmosphere. And the choice to record at Musicland was inspired, as nobody bothered them and they could live relatively normal lives.

They were also impressed by Reinhold Mack, the resident engineer/producer at Musicland. It was the first time Queen had gone into the recording studio without any schedule or deadline, or a favoured engineer or producer. They planned to rehearse and record new material without any pressure. No fixed structure of which member supplied their allotted songs for an album.

The direction given to Mack was to make it fresh and exciting. He did and was given co-producer credit for what became *The Game* album.

Landing at Munchen-Riem airport, a local driver with a large Mercedes whisked us to the Hilton hotel. Freddie never learned to drive, and had no interest in doing so. He was a rock star and stars were driven, so they could concentrate on being creative and wonderful. Arriving at his hotel suite (always the biggest and grandest available) Freddie wanted to freshen up and take a bath. While he did, I was instructed to call the studio and inform them that 'his self' was back.

I complied. While chatting with Fred's driver, I heard noises coming from the bathroom. Mr Mercury was muttering and humming. Then he called out, using my nickname, 'Ratty':

'Ratty! Come here, come here!'

'Fred, you want me to come into your bathroom…?'

Freddie appeared in the doorway wearing a towelling robe, still wet and dripping.

'No! Just get me a guitar, I need a guitar, now!'

I pulled out an old scratchy acoustic guitar from under a sofa, but before I could check it was in tune he snatched it from me. He meant business. Fred started playing D, G and C chords. As he tapped the guitar rhythmically with his hand and drew inspiration from somewhere only geniuses like Freddie Mercury can. He had this habit of waving his hands by the side of his head as though they were antenna tuning into some unknown force. He found it.

'Right! Call the studio, tell them to stop everything, I'm coming and we'll record this now!'

I did as I was told.

I don't recall Freddie making any written notes, but when we got to the studio he was a combination of focused and frantic. He had to capture and tame the creative creature he had unleashed, before it escaped forever. He played the song on a far superior Martin acoustic guitar to John Deacon and Roger Taylor, who loved the idea and immediately started work on the backing track.

'What's it called then Fred?'

'Crazy Little Thing Called Love.'

It's remarkable that I witnessed first-hand the birth and nurturing of one of Queen's biggest hits, which happened in just a couple of hours. But I was in the presence of a genius. And I don't use the term lightly.

The song was a new direction for Queen, who were renowned for their complex arrangements, experimental sounds and lavish production. 'Crazy' was a back-to-basics, stripped down composition that referenced early rock 'n' roll and Elvis Presley.

Mack advised Brian May to play the lead guitar break on a Fender Telecaster, rather than on the cherished homemade guitar that he had used throughout his career. The Fender Telecaster epitomised the 1950s era and sound. It worked perfectly.

Sometime later I convinced Freddie to change from a 12-string acoustic guitar and play a white Fender Telecaster on stage for 'Crazy'. He liked white costumes on stage as it focused the audience on him, even from the back of a 20,000 seat arena. And a white guitar worked too – he looked far better throwing guitar hero poses with solid electric than on an acoustic guitar.

'Crazy' was released as a single and an immediate hit, giving Queen their first number one in America, before the album was even finished.

The '79–'80 Munich sessions that became *The Game* album were a watershed for Queen, when they morphed from being a successful, somewhat heavy rock band into a hugely successful commercial rock band with international fame and countless hit singles and albums in every territory. Reinhold Mack was an important factor in pushing Queen onto a new level of success and musical styles and experimentation. Timing is so important in life and especially in careers. Fate? Luck? Queen worked exceptionally hard and had belief in the ethos that 'quality and style will always shine through, darling'.

However, despite the huge success generated in Munich, it was also subsequently where the excess began to creep in. The pressures of being in a big band are huge. Another album to do and it must be bigger and better than the last one. Queen were four human beings with all the temptations, weaknesses and desires of anybody else. They needed to relax from the constant reminder of always having to deliver – and also from the fear of losing all that they had achieved. No band ever really knows how long it will last, they just hope, keep working and keep going.

Sex and drugs and rock 'n' roll. And alcohol of course.

Not that there weren't more relaxed moments, too. Recording studios can be dull, dreary, prosaic places to spend time when you are not directly involved in the creative process, so entertainment is required. Queen are known for their love of playing Scrabble, Freddie in particular, so I was sent out to buy a boxed set. 'Now, do it now!' (A phrase Mr Mercury often quoted.) But of course the only Scrabble set at the Munich games emporium I tracked down was a German version, which did not amuse Fred.

'What can I do with all these fucking zeds and umlauts? Make words like "zimmer frame", "Obergruppenführer" or "Volkswagen"? Get me a proper Scrabble set!'

So, at some expense, an English edition was couriered from London. If only we had the immediate luxury back then of the internet to Google what was required and then have it delivered.

Fred would often stop work to play Scrabble or interfere in another game and insist he help, or that we scrapped the game and started another so he could play – and often win. He didn't like losing but would get very excited at clever play and interesting words. I recall we had a version of the game where only swear words, filthy terms, slang or general sex words were allowed.

Musicland had a VCR – video recorder. Remember those? Again, Fred would want to watch the bits of a film or shows he liked and one in particular was a diner scene in *The Blues Brothers* with Aretha Franklin. The Blues Brothers come in to recruit Matt 'guitar' Murphy, as they are putting the band together again. Mrs Murphy (Aretha Franklin) is not happy and tells him 'You're not going back on the road no more and you ain't playing any more two-bit sleazy dives!' The scene segues into a wonderful version of 'Think' as people dance around the diner. Fred loved that phrase, 'Two-bit sleazy dives' and the way she delivered it. He would quote it while impersonating Aretha. Then slap the table or his thigh, saying 'What a line, God I wish I'd written that!'

Musicland also offered a great pinball machine, other board games and a table tennis table in the underground corridor outside the kitchen, which is where I took various portraits of the band.

Fred would joyfully take on anybody and beat them at table tennis, often with one hand behind his back. There are times when you want to hate people who have so much talent – but then Fred couldn't make a cup of tea, wire a plug or load a truck...

"It was the first time Queen had gone into the recording studio without any schedule or deadline, or a favoured engineer or producer. They planned to rehearse and record new material without any pressure."

Above: When in Munich... In a beer garden. Brian is holding one of his collection of stereo cameras. Roger has my Hasselblad 500 CM camera.

Opposite above: The view from the balcony of the Hilton hotel, showing the Olympic Park and Tower, built for the 1976 Olympic Games.

Opposite below: The graphic exterior of the Arabellahaus hotel. Musicland was in the basement.

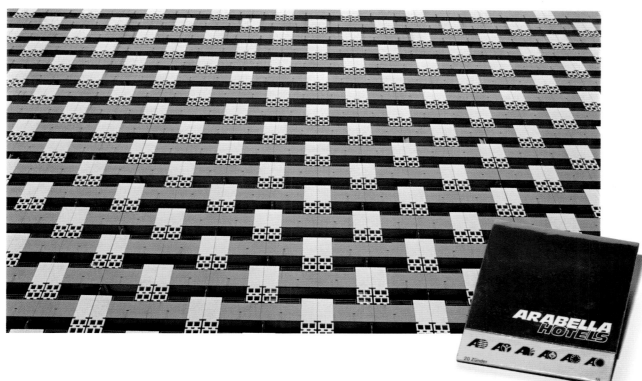

FREDDIE'S DEBUT

Freddie's moustache became his trademark look in the 1980s.
This Polaroid is the very first picture of him sporting it and
was taken in the dining area of Musicland in 1980, during *The
Game* sessions. I had recently brought a Polaroid back for my
Hasselblad camera and Fred asked me to take a picture of
him so he could see how he looked in print form. As I waited
the standard sixty seconds for the Polaroid to develop, Fred
became agitated. 'Come on, how much longer?'

  I peeled the backing off and before I could take a good look,
he snatched it from me, purring 'I look great, don't I!' The jury
was still out on that... However, it became his trademark for most
of the 1980s, despite fans throwing disposable razors onstage
in protest.

Above: The kitchen and two dining and hanging-out areas at Musicland. In the bottom right I'm researching, using an ancient codex, most likely die Gelbe Seiten (yellow pages) telephone directory, to source an establishment or service. Google? Sounds like a 1980s guitar effects pedal...

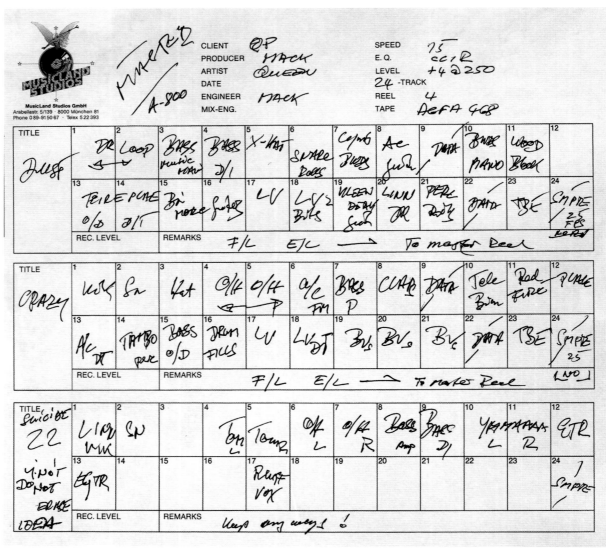

Opposite: John and Mack working on 'Another One Bites The Dust'. John is looking at notes on a 24-track sheet, where the details of what instruments, vocals, etc, were allocated and logged. Likely very similar to the one above.

Above: Brian with his homemade Red Special guitar, looking toward the control room.

PLAY THE GAME

I had been asked to do some photos of the band and posed them collectively and individually on a balcony of the Munich Hilton, where we stayed. I had been experimenting with Cokin, graduated tone filters that could be raised or lowered in front of the lens to give colour in the sky or foreground, the top or the bottom of the picture. I used them on some of the band shots and then also while taking photos of water from the Eisbach river that ran alongside the Hilton. At one point it drops over a small weir and I used the filters for effect. When all the processed film was laid out on a light box for the band to view, Fred felt that there was not much colour tone in his shots – but when he saw the toned water images, he picked them up and arranged some behind band photos. 'That's it!'

And so it was. In the days before Photoshop the band were 'comped' with the toned water background. People think that it's fire, but it's the opposite element, water. However, when Queen filmed the video for 'Play The Game' they used a blue screen background and fire was inserted.

THE SUGAR SHACK

The Sugar Shack was a Munich nightclub that attracted a strong rock 'n' roll audience. It played album tracks and very few singles – continuously, with no interruption or 'talk' from the DJ. The sound system was tremendous and gave the rock tracks real power. I've never heard a better sounding or arranged sound system in a club or disco. And, of course, it was very loud.

In fact, some Queen tracks were debuted at the Sugar Shack, before they were heard anywhere else. 'Another One Bites The Dust' was one example. Producer Mack gave the DJ a cassette to play and then carefully monitored the sound and the security of the cassette. As a lot of the material played in the Shack was by bands we'd never heard of, it was interesting to gauge people's reactions to a song without them having any idea who it was by.

Right: Before going into the studio outside London, I would ask John, Brian and Roger what instruments (aside from drums, which his roadie organised) they wanted to take with them. Roger had a big collection of older guitars, now termed 'Classic' or 'Vintage'. It was important to have options in the studio in order to get a particular sound. It was on one of Roger's Telecasters that Brian played the lead break for 'Crazy Little Thing Called Love'. The black Telecaster that Brian subsequently played on 'Crazy' for live shows was bought by me for the song's video from Rose-Morris music shop on Shaftesbury Avenue. The Ovation 12-string guitars Queen played also came from Rose-Morris.

Above: Breakfast was usually served somewhere between 2pm and 5pm and to whoever had showed up. Rarely did the band eat breakfast all together, but they did sit around the dinner table en masse in the evening – which was effectively lunch...

Left: Fred and Mack working on one of Fred's songs for *Hot Space* in 1981. Fred is playing air guitar to demonstrate what he wants.

Above: The band run through a backing track in the studio.

FRED WITH AUGUSTINER

I was taking some portraits of the band for Japan's *Music Life* magazine and set up in the underground corridor outside Musicland. After doing somewhat standard shots against background paper Fred said, 'Come on, I want you to make me look mean and tough.'
He moved to the adjacent scruffy wall and I changed the lighting. Fred had been playing the 'tough guy' role, when he suddenly dropped his head as if to contemplate something. I got the shot and it's one of my favourite images of him. He has a vulnerable look, despite the leather jacket, and holds a beer bottle in a rather phallic manner.
The beer is Augustiner – *the* beer of Munich since 1328. The significance of Augustiner meant nothing to me until I recently held an exhibition at Munich's Galerie Stephen Hoffman to celebrate Queen and just how important the city was for them.
My partner Karin, who is Munich born and bred, excitedly pointed out when I showed her the print, 'But it's an Augustiner!'
It's such an iconic beer in Bavaria they don't even advertise it, but the directors of Augustiner now have personal signed copies of that print. Thank you Musicland Studios for stocking Augustiner as their house beer!

Roger was always somebody who wanted to try new ideas, play around with things and have fun. The 'Drums' sticker on his forehead was one of several used to identify equipment, along with colour codes on the flight cases. We had Piano (to include all keyboards) stickers, which were yellow, pink for Guitar, blue for Bass, and green for dressing room. And drums were identifiable by red flight cases, so the background to this shot synchs perfectly.

The one photo I wish I had suggested to all four members of the band was to have their respective instrument stickers attached to their foreheads and to pose with deadpan expressions. Oh, the wonder of hindsight.

UNION STUDIOS

John and I flew to Munich so he could mix the
12-inch edition of 'I Want to Break Free', but Musicland
was booked – Spandau Ballet were in. Instead, Mack
booked Union Studios and the subsequent mix, with
its slowly building synth intro, proved so popular
that it became the one used for the original seven-
inch single. The only occasion any Queen project in
Munich was done outside of Musicland Studios.

Life in Munich. We generally spent our time there in winter and, due to the hours we kept and working in a basement, rarely saw daylight. Below is a Deutschmark from 1979, the year Queen first recorded in the city. A reminder of a bygone era, before the Euro, when Europe had so many different currencies.

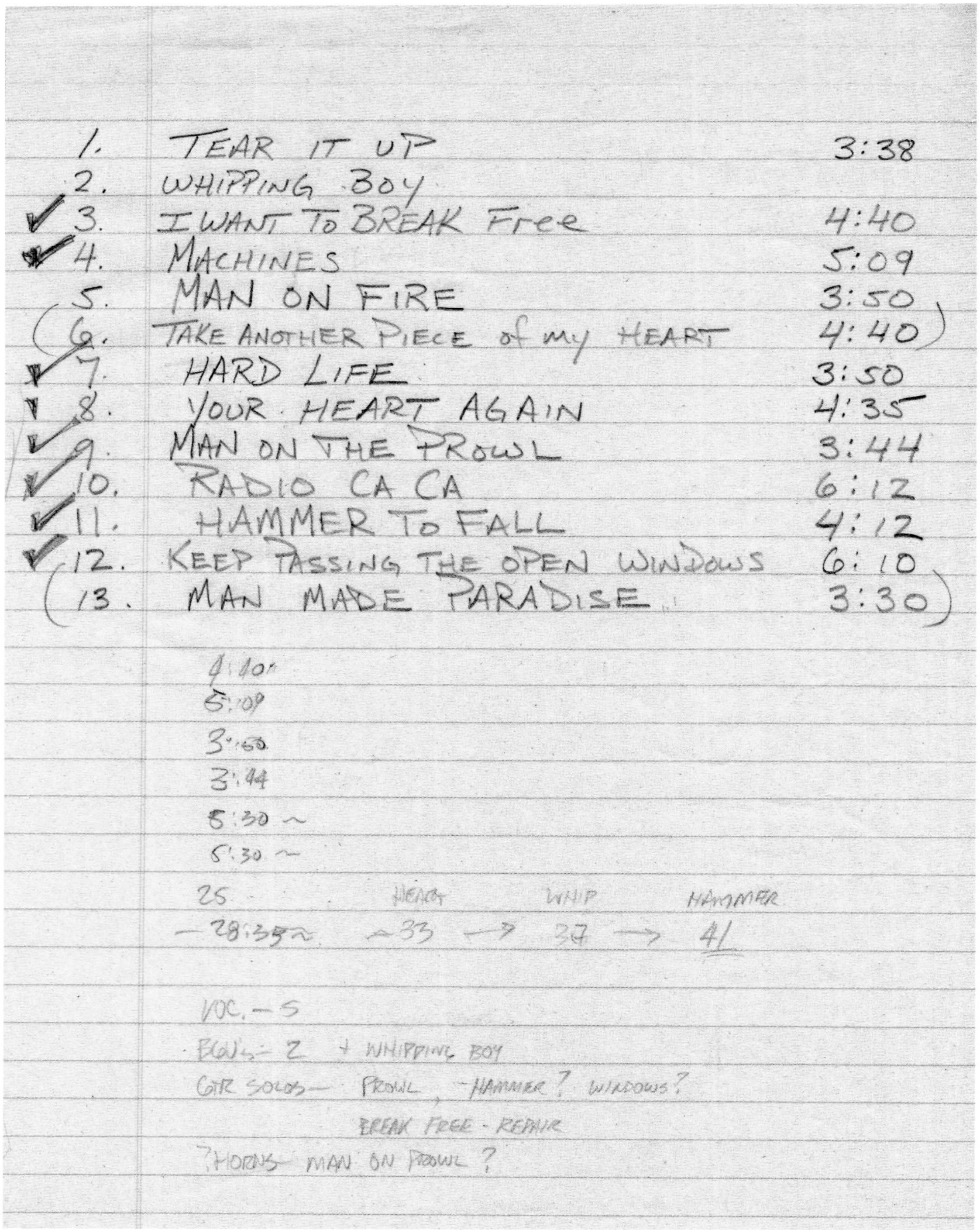

	1.	TEAR IT UP	3:38
	2.	WHIPPING BOY	
✔	3.	I WANT TO BREAK Free	4:40
✔	4.	MACHINES	5:09
	5.	MAN ON FIRE	3:50
(	6.	TAKE ANOTHER PIECE of MY HEART	4:40)
✔	7.	HARD LIFE	3:50
✔	8.	YOUR HEART AGAIN	4:35
✔	9.	MAN ON THE PROWL	3:44
✔	10.	RADIO CA CA	6:12
✔	11.	HAMMER TO FALL	4:12
✔	12.	KEEP PASSING THE OPEN WINDOWS	6:10
(	13.	MAN MADE PARADISE	3:30)

4:40
5:09
3:50
3:44
5:30 ~
5:30 ~

25.   HEART   WHIP   HAMMER
— 28:35~   ~33   →   37   →   41

VOC. — 5
BGVs — 2   + WHIPPING BOY
GTR SOLOS — PROWL , HAMMER? WINDOWS?
              BREAK FREE - REPAIR
? HORNS — MAN ON PROWL ?

Above: An early running order track list for *The Works*, with notes of
times, etc. The final album was quite different.

CHAPTER 4
JAPAN

Japan was the exotic rock 'n' roll destination that few bands in the mid 1970s had visited.

In the roadie hierarchy there was a certain kudos to be had from touring America, but to have done shows in Japan back then was to reach the rock 'n' roll heights of Mount Fuji.

Tokyo was intriguing, exciting, bewildering and the most alien place I'd ever been. A bombardment of colour and visuals, tempered with serenity and calm. In Europe you could have a try at pronouncing words in different languages, but in Japan you felt truly in need of help, somewhat lost. So when travelling, the hotel or interpreter would supply you with written instructions for a taxi driver or train station ticket office.

The vibrant neon explosion of displays in the cities excited the senses along with the smells of street food and even the fragrance of hotel soap still holds strong in the memory. It was palpable we were in the extraordinary east. I would buy kimonos, woodblock prints, ceramics and other examples of Japanese art and graphics to take home as souvenirs. Fred adored Japan and would buy all manner of art – and leave it to me to ship it home for him.

Japanese culture was not what we were used to; people were polite and courteous and etiquette was paramount, so lewd, rude roadie behaviour was not acceptable. Paradoxically, there were some disturbingly graphic magazines on general sale, despite Penthouse and Playboy being censored, by hand with felt tip pens.

Ceremony and ritual were important and a firm policy of how fans should behave at rock concerts was in place. Shows started at 6 or 6.30pm, with no support act. On early tours we played matinees at 2pm as well as the later shows. Queen were matinee idols! The Japanese custom of bowing was intriguing and a handful of the crew tested this ritual by coming on stage and bowing to the audience prior to a show. Some people in the front rows responded. When we bowed again, more bowed back, then like a Mexican wave it spread. Realising we were joking people politely giggled behind their hands and smiled, even applauded us. Some nights we went down better than the band...

One of the finest venues in Japan was the Nippon Budokan. The famous indoor arena within the boundaries of the Imperial Palace hosted sumo wrestling along with countless rock shows, ranging from The Beatles to ZZ Top. It is a favourite of so many rock bands that several live albums have been recorded there. However, there were restrictions that affected big live productions. There was a low weight limit on what could be hung from certain points in the roof, so scaffold towers had to be built to accommodate some of Queen's huge lighting rigs. No pyrotechnics were allowed and exits and gangways had to be lit; there was no real blackout to heighten the drama before a band take the stage. In other countries these rules and regulations could be bent to accommodate everybody happily, but not in Japan.

A BUDOKAN BONUS

A 1976 bonus envelope from the Budokan arena in Tokyo. When the Budokan was sold out everybody involved in the production received a percentage bonus – usually about £2 in old money – presented to us in these envelopes

```
                    ITINERARY FOR THE CREW

          QUEEN JAPAN TOUR - 1979

     Thursday, April 12

     12:00  pick up equipment at the customs of Yokohama Port

     15:00  arrive at Budokan
            start welding, etc.

     18:00  load in, and start setting up
            (power supply of the house cannot be used)

     22:00  lighting

     Friday, April 13   18:30  Concert at Budokan(03-216-0781)
                               capacity - 9000

     7:30   pick-up for hall from Shibuya Tokyu Inn(03-498-0109)

     8:00   P.A. and band equipment

     13:00  sound check

     17:00  doors open

     18:30  show time

     20:30  show ends, return to hotel

     Saturday, April 14   18:30  Concert at Budokan(03-216-0781)

            decide the time of sound check after we have seen how
            work has gone in the previous day.

     17:30  doors open

     18:30  show time

     20:30  show ends
            load out
            return to hotel
```

Peter Hince

FREDDIE THE ENTERTAINER

Fred, always spontaneous during shows, chose to make his
entry for the encore in 1979 on the shoulders of Superman
(more commonly known as security man Paul, dressed up
in costume). But on one occasion in Tokyo he decided to
wear a bunch of bananas on his head, then throw them
individually to the audience.

The 1979 tour. **Above:** A group shot of band, crew and Japanese staff onstage at the Budokan.
Below: A celebratory Korean barbecue meal for band and crew. Freddie is flanked by his partner, Joe Fanelli, and Mary Austin, his long-term girlfriend and closest confidant.

THE CHAMPIONS

This is one of my favourite images and a view I saw
countless times during 'We Are The Champions'. I
saw many wonderful visual opportunities during live
perfomances but my tasks were to monitor Fred and
John, execute my many cues and do my job as a roadie.
But this image I just had to capture.

I had long wanted to do an overhead shot of the band on stage, so I took these images using a custom adapted remote control cable attached to a motor drive on a Nikon 35mm camera fitted with a wide angle 20mm lens I had just bought. I set it up at the back of the lighting rig to cover the stage and some of the audience. Choosing my times during the show carefully, I fired off the frames. I only had one 36-exposure film and had to judge exposure and view carefully – the fact the lighting rig moved didn't help! I also used the same set-up on one of the onstage spotlight units on stage right. The results were very pleasing and are unique; nobody else has these views of the band on stage.

The 1982 end of tour party at Sapporo Beer Gardens with band, crew and Japanese staff. Trip Khalaf, Queen's live sound engineer, sits alongside Fred. A beer-drinking contest ensued – Brian can be seen holding his own. John Deacon is with Wardrobe Master Tony 'Mr Hyde' Williams. Squeezed in the centre is lighting designer Jimmy Barnett.

Above: Roger, felt-tip pen in hand, in a more sober, prosaic environment, drinking coffee in a dressing room as he plies through a thick ream of gilt-edged cards to be signed for Japanese dignitaries and guests. Platters of cling-filmed sandwiches were laid on for added sustenance.

VISA APPLICATION FORM TO ENTER JAPAN

Name in full   Hince
         Peter Raymond   (Surname)
                              (Given and middle name)
Different name used, if any
Sex   Male   Marital status   married   single   XXXXX
Nationality or citizenship   British
Former nationality, if any
Date and place of birth   23   Jan   55 : Hereford   England
                        (Day) (Month) (Year) (City)   (Province)   (Country)
Criminal record, if any
Home address   46 Pembridge Road
         London England   Tel. 727-5641
Profession or occupation   Head Technician
Name and address of firm or organization to which applicant belongs   GLS Management Services, Inc.
1040 N. Las Palmas, Hollywood, California   Tel.   (213)462-7101
Post or rank held at present
Principal former positions
Passport   (Refugee or stateless should note the title of Travel Document)
   No.   590139D   Diplomatic, Official, Ordinary Issued at   London   on 7/13/82
   Issuing authority   British Consul   Valid until   07/13/82
Purpose of journey to Japan   Performance by Contract
Length of stay in Japan intended   3 weeks
Route of present journey : Name of ship or airline   Japan Airlines
   Port of entry into Japan   Tokyo   Probable date of entry 6 May 1985
Address of hotels or names and addresses of persons with whom applicant intends to stay
New Otani, Kioi-cho, Chiyoda ku, Tokyo Japan
Dates and duration of previous stays in Japan   November 1982   2 weeks
Guarantor or reference in Japan : Name Watanabe Productions, Ltd., Kaisei Bldg,
   Address   1-8-10 Azabudai, Minato Ku Japan   Tel. 502-0541
Relationship to applicant
Persons accompanying applicant   Name   Relationship   Birthdate
and included in his passport

I hereby declare that the statement given above is true and correct. Also, I understand that immigration status and period of stay to be granted are decided by the Japanese immigration authorities upon my arrival.
Date of application   21/3/85
                        Signature of applicant
(FORM No. 1-C)

"Japanese culture was not
what we were used to;
people were polite and
courteous and etiquette was
paramount."

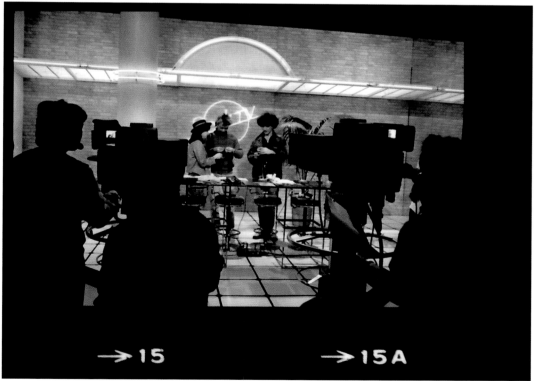

QUEEN IN KOREA

All I knew about Korea was they had a war in the 1950s and the popular TV comedy M*A*S*H was set there – although the series was actually filmed in Malibu state park on the outskirts of Los Angeles. In 1984, I accompanied John Deacon on a promotional tour for The Works album, along with Roger Taylor and his assistant Crystal. We flew to Japan, on to Hong Kong and then to Seoul in South Korea for a succession of press and TV interviews by very excitable journalists. There had been discussions on doing shows in Korea, so we visited the stadium and arenas that were already completed for the upcoming 1988 Olympic Games. Sadly Queen never got play the country.

CHAPTER 5

MONTREUX

Queen first visited Montreux in 1978, the starting point for a year out of Britain for tax purposes. The picturesque chocolate box town was home to Mountain Studios.

Other big rock bands had recorded there, so it had a good reputation. However, the tranquil town on the lake did not have a reputation for rock 'n' roll rowdiness – in fact, the police took down all of our details and watched us closely while we resided there.

The band had driven over from London and brought their families and children with them, so they were somewhat residential and domestic. However, for the rest of us, if there was fun to be found we would find it!

Rehearsals started at a small ballet school on summer break, where Fred's Steinway piano – weighing in at over a tonne in its enormous flight case – badly damaged an antique parquet floor. Much to the horror of the studio staff, who had only obtained the use of the ballet school on the premise it was for a quartet of musicians doing a little practice.

We moved on from pirouettes and guitar pyrotechnics to the Montreux Casino building, taking over exclusive use of a section of the salon, an area of the building that housed the annual jazz festival, which we'd attended during rehearsals. The scale of this can be seen in the panoramic photo I took for the inside gatefold of the album *Jazz*.

After a two-album break, Queen had brought producer Roy Thomas Baker back, and it would be the first Queen album where they had not used engineer Mike Stone. Roy was working with a fine engineer, Geoff Workman, and they had recently had huge success with Boston band The Cars' first album for Elektra, coincidentally Queen's record company in the USA.

Roy had insisted that the bass drum of Roger's kit was placed exactly centrally in the vast space of the salon. Using a formula that utilised bits of string, a weight and some guesswork, this was

achieved. The guitar and piano were housed in separation booths to avoid leakage and keep the individual sounds clean.

Mountain Studios was unusual in having no direct visual communication between the control room and the studio. Most studios had wide multi-glazed windows so the studio team could give a wave, a thumbs up, a nod or even a rude gesture to the musicians who had headphones clamped on. Mountain used CCTV cameras for the small permanent studio above the control room and also for the large salon Queen used for the *Jazz* album. Two TV monitor screens were set into the wall opposite where the engineer and producer sat at the console.

It gave a sense of communication, but for the band they must have felt somewhat isolated and it took a while for them to get into the mindset of responding to directions in their headphones as they played in an unusual setting. Even the vast Abbey Road studio, where the Beatles did so much of their work and could house whole orchestras, had a window to look up to where George Martin, or whoever it may be, would appear – in person.

Queen returned to Montreux in spring 1979 after a European tour that had been recorded every night by the Manor Mobile portable recording studio. The countless tapes were painstakingly reviewed as shortlists were made for the tracklisting. The result of the mixing, tweaking and a few subtle overdubs was the *Live Killers* double album. Queen were always a great live act with powerful visual appeal – but could the sonic alone create the same atmosphere? It's a difficult ask.

Initially, each member would work on their own songs and then collaborate with each other and engineer John Etchells, who they had worked with at Superbear studios in France the year before.

After taking ownership of Mountain Studios, Queen only used it briefly in my time with them, a short spell in early autumn 1981 during the recording of *Hot Space*. But that short spell did produce one of Queen's greatest ever songs and a huge hit: 'Under Pressure'.

Having worked for David Bowie in the early 1970s, I was familiar with his working methods and personality. Undoubtedly a genius, a true artist who expressed himself through music, film, art, mime and performance, David, along with Fred, was one of those people who had an aura. You immediately felt it when they walked into the room, a feeling of slight intimidation but also excitement to be in the presence of somebody special. David was spontaneous, driven and very much his own man. Like Queen, he knew what he wanted and put in the hard work and persistence to achieve his success. In the Ziggy Stardust and the Spiders from Mars days he had the luxury of working with another genius, guitarist Mick Ronson, who was instrumental in the sound that consolidated the success. 'Ronno' was a classically trained musician on piano, recorder and violin, but could master any instrument. His arrangement and production skills are vastly underrated. He co-produced, arranged tracks and played on Lou Reed's *Transformer* album, recorded at the same Trident Studios in Soho as 'Ziggy Stardust' – and where early Queen albums were also recorded.

At the time Queen were in Montreux, David Bowie was living in nearby Vevey and had used Mountain Studios for his own projects, utilising David Richards, the house engineer and producer. Through the grapevine it became evident that David would like to drop by and say hello to Queen. I'm not sure if any of them had ever met before, but Roger was a huge fan of David's.

Mr Bowie popped in and a greeting of mutual respect took place; the shaking of hands, nodding of heads. Then Fred took the lead, inviting David to stay, have a drink – and then he played him some of the new Queen tracks.

The mood was convivial and they decided to jam in the top studio. They played classics, rock 'n' roll songs, Free hits, the Stones, Mott The Hoople's 'All The Young Dudes' (written by David) and some of each other's songs too. It was all very loose and relaxed, but something definitely clicked.

John had a riff, he played it and the others followed. It was the classic introduction to 'Under Pressure'. There is a story in circulation that everybody then went out for a pizza and, on returning to the studio, found that John had forgotten the riff. I don't recall exactly the events of the evening, but find it unlikely John would do that. After playing around with the riff and ideas for this new song, it was agreed that they were on to something special and should return the next day and record it properly.

Other tracks were written ad hoc and recorded. David also added vocals to some of Queen's existing *Hot Space* songs. And when they were jamming the tape was rolling. Did this material get erased? Will the other songs ever be released? I imagine they are locked in some James Bond villain-style vault in the Swiss mountains – perhaps. As David and Freddie are sadly no longer with us and John not actively part of Queen anymore, no doubt there are issues of ownership and the involvement of estates to overcome before the public get to hear this magical music. But we live in hope.

MONTREUX
ET ENVIRONS

PLAN Officiel et Guide   Fr. 6.80

Editions de la Veveyse – av. gare, 21 – Vevey

White Horse Pub
MONTREUX

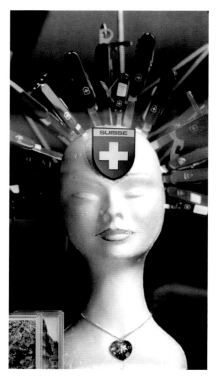

SUISSE

12. International
JAZZ Festival

july 7/23 juillet/1978
Switzerland

MONTREUX
JAZZ

SÃO PAULO

1º Festival Internacional de JAZZ
Brasil
11/18 de setembro/1978

MONTREUX
INTERNATIONAL FESTIVAL

Above: The map given to me when I first arrived in Montreux, with useful reference points marked, including 'Fred's Gaff', an imposing mountainside villa dubbed 'Pink Mansions'.

Right, above: The band pose with the backdrop of Lac Leman and the French Alps as a local cruiser passes.

Right below and overleaf: A promotional garden party held by the record company in the gardens of the Eden Au Lac Hotel on the lakefront. At the wine glass strewn table to the right are (L–R): Roger, Chrissy May, PR man Tony Brainsby, Brian, producer Roy Thomas-Baker and Mary Austin.

BALLET SCHOOL

The only known image of Queen rehearsing in the ballet school in Montreux, where Fred's Steinway piano caused serious damage to the precious floor. As well as that there was the noise level, another issue that shook both the Alps and the locals, when Brian cranked up his Red Special guitar through a Mesa Boogie Amp. Or his trusted AC30s. I recall 'Don't Stop Me Now' being one of the first songs to be worked on.

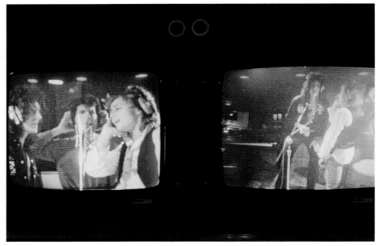

EMI EMI RECORDING STUDIOS, 3 ABBEY RD., LONDON, NW8 9AY. Tel: 01-286 1161

Client

Artist *Queen*

Studio   Engineer   Date

Matrix No YAX-5550   Job No   Tape Length 20'52

"JAZZ ALBUM"

SIDE 1

1	Mustapha	3.05
2	Fat bottomed Girls	4.12
3	Jealousy	3.15
4	Bicycle Race	3.05
5	If You can't beat them	4.17
6	Let me Entertain you.	3.02

DOLBY 'A' ENCODED
TONES at START recorded with 'NR' OUT
1kHz, 5kHz, 10kHz and 60Hz at – 4VU
(0VU = 320 nWb/m) then DOLBY TONE
ON REPLAY SET DOLBY TONE TO NAB

| A | Recording Date: | Noise Reduction ☐ Yes ☐ No | B |

SIDE ONE

1. Mustapha	3:05
2. Fat Bottomed Girls	4:12
3. Jealousy	3:15
4. Bicycle Race	3:05
5. If You Can't Beat Them	4:17
6. Let Me Entertain You	3:02

SIDE TWO

1. Dead On Time	3:28
2. In Only Seven Days	2:27
3. Dreamers Ball	3:30
4. Fun It	3:18

QUEEN   maxell UD

5. Leaving Home Ain't Easy	3:13
6. Don't Stop Me Now	3:44
7. (More Of That) Jazz	4:13

Left: Scenes from the studio and the Montreux Casino salon.

Above: A ¼-inch stereo tape box of *Jazz*, which albums were cut from, and a final cassette of the album with tracks and timings. The tape reel is a typical 24-track tape.

SWITZERLAND
930 - Le Cervin
Matterhorn (4 477 m)

Above and overleaf: Unseen panoramic shots. A similar one to the photograph overleaf was used for the gatefold of *Jazz*. All taken on a rented 35mm Widelux camera, usually employed to capture large groups of people such as school or college class photographs, military academy graduates, etc. A very basic camera with limited settings but gives an impressive result.

Working on the mix of *Live Killers* in the control room at Mountain Studios,
trying to capture the incredible Queen live show with sound alone.

"Initially, each member would work on their own songs and then collaborate with each other and engineer John Etchells."

Left: Brian on a synthesiser, in the control room during recording for *Hot Space* in 1981. Queen made a point of stating 'No synthesisers' on their album sleeve notes until *The Game*. Roger had bought an Oberheim OBX polyphonic synth and it was first used by the band in Munich. It featured on several tracks to break the mould, as Queen's music developed, a pattern they followed in Montreux.

Fred turns to camera while working on *Hot Space* in 1981. The CCTV monitors show how visual contact was maintained between the control room and the studio.

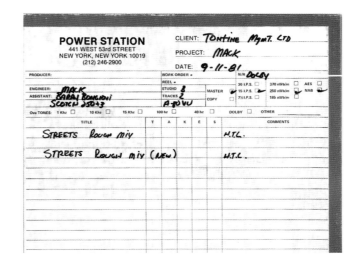

QUEEN AND DAVID BOWIE

'Under Pressure' was done quite spontaneously and the result is, in my opinion, one of Queen's best songs. John maintained it was one of the best things they did as a band and Roger of course was delighted with the collaboration.

The original title was 'People on Streets', as you can see from the notes in the cassette case above. It was changed to 'Under Pressure' in New York while mixing, attended by Freddie, Bowie, Mack and, I think, Roger. Some vocals and lyrics were also changed at this stage.

David did direct proceedings to a degree, which Queen weren't used to; an outsider. But the compromise and different working style brought great results.

Top left: A cassette containing a rough mix of 'People on Streets', which later became 'Under Pressure'.

Left: A VHS of the 'Under Pressure' video, produced using historical stock footage and directed by David Mallet, who had already directed videos for Bowie. The first cut was banned due to supposedly unsuitable political imagery and re-edited for broadcast.

Above: The studio room of Mountain Studios in Montreux.

Below: Roger listens to a Walkman during the 'Under Pressure'/*Hot Space* sessions, in a rest area on the balcony outside the control room. The Sony Walkman revolutionised how people listened to music and also how musicians wrote and recorded. It was a great device for popping in a demo cassette or backing track, to take notes and develop songs. Here Roger uses one of the original models.

SUPER BEAR

Super Bear Studios was based in the tiny French village of
Berre-les-Alpes, an hour's drive up hairpin roads into the hills
north of Nice. This is where the final overdubs and mixing
of *Jazz* were done. It was a residential studio, with other
accommodation provided nearby. The photograph above
shows the front of the building, with producer Roy Thomas
Baker riding a mini, fold-up motorbike. Engineer Geoff
Workman and Brian look on.

CHAPTER 6

SOUTH AMERICA

Who dares wins.
South America was where the good drugs came from, but nobody would seriously consider touring there.

At the time it was seen as too unstable, dangerous, to risk it would be simply throwing money to the wind. It was wilder than the Wild West, with plenty of cowboys. Or gauchos.

Stories circulated about major bands who had attempted to tour in South America, only to have their equipment impounded or stolen. Receiving payment was a nebulous area that nobody had a direct answer to, apart from the regular response, 'Manana'.

So paying heed to all of this caution, Queen chose to go, a case of all for one and one for all! Pioneering spirit. Queen were always up for a new challenge and fortunately it came at the right time, as they were on top of the world in early 1981. *The Game* album had taken them exactly where they wanted to be. For those precious, fleeting moments they were the biggest band on the planet.

Tour manager Gerry Stickells was instrumental, not only in negotiations but in overseeing the whole operation and actually making it happen. But, paradoxically, we also made it up as we went along, as venues and dates were changed or cancelled and extra shows added. It kept us on our toes. Queen unquestionably paved the way for other rock bands to tour in South America.

Communication, essential to touring, was often difficult. Language barriers, cultural issues and people who simply lied through their teeth to you. It was far more difficult and much harder work than any other touring experiences. Even overseas phone calls had to be booked through the hotel switchboard and often a line was not clear for an hour or more.

Anticipating that there would be technical and production issues, Queen shipped virtually everything needed to put on a show. The lighting, sound system and Queen's own equipment was air freighted from Tokyo and all staging, towers and electrical supply hook-up came by sea container. All we needed was enough power to hook-up to. It was to prove a wise piece of foresight.

Playing in outdoor stadiums brought a variety of new challenges, particularly tuning issues. All guitars and the OBXa synthesisers were tuned to the reference point of Fred's Steinway grand piano. Once that had been tuned, I would take a reading on an electronic strobe tuner – and all the other tuners used by Brian, his roadie, John and me were then calibrated to the same A440 pitch. Sometimes it may be a cent or two sharp/flat, sometimes spot-on, all the individual tuners having been collectively set up and calibrated at the start of the tour. Heat and humidity were the biggest problems. A piano that is tuned in the hot afternoon will not be in tune at around midnight, when some shows started. The drop in temperature will make some strings sharp, while humidity will lower them. So the piano was tuned before soundcheck and then again as close as possible to the band taking the stage. The same for guitars; I tuned all John's and Fred's on the stage, in the same environment that they would be played.

All the hard work was rewarded in witnessing Queen play to vast crowds that broke world records for paying audiences. The response from the fans was phenomenal, the energy they transmitted was palpable onstage, which Queen utlised to give some of the best performances of their career.

The tour started in Buenos Aires, Argentina. The football stadiums we played in were impressive as they had been recently updated for the 1978 World Cup. During a Buenos Aires show, a young curly-haired footballer was brought onstage and introduced, receiving wild response from the crowd. The short 20-year-old was none other than Diego Maradona, already a huge hero in Argentina,

having made his full international debut at just 16 years old – but generally unheard of in Europe at the time. The other cities played in Argentina were Mar Del Plata and Rosario, with a triumphant return to Buenos Aires at the end.

Brazil followed Argentina with a lot of 'TBA' days in the itinerary: 'To Be Advised/Arranged', though it was more a case of 'To Be Avoided' as plans chopped and changed regularly. The band were initially due to play Rio De Janeiro, but the Maracana stadium was deemed worthy of hosting performances only by the holy trinity of the Pope, Frank Sinatra and football, so the show didn't happen. Belo Horizonte was cancelled for reasons I don't recall, so we ended up playing just two shows, at Morumbi stadium in São Paulo. That was, however, to a total of 251,000 people, a world record attendance for a paying audience.

The two tours in 1981 gave Queen incredible highs playing to fanatical audiences. Later that year they extended their reach to include Venezuela and Mexico. This was, however, probably the lowest point of the tour, particularly Mexico, where ticketless, tequila-fuelled fans stormed the gates and broke into the stadium early in the day. During the first show the stage was pelted with bottles, batteries, other injurious objects – and shoes for some reason – all in the name of appreciation, apparently. The second show saw fans searched and batteries removed from cassette recorders, only to be available for sale inside the stadium, at a stall set-up by security... We opted to veto the third show and, on the day off before it, escaped by the skin of our teeth, and with a US dollar loss running into seven figures.

As a crew we were road hardened and streetwise, but the dangers in South America were not always apparent – but very real.

Fortunately, we had some degree of protection due to our status, despite being in military-run states, where people disappeared for opposing authority. There is no question in my mind that permission for Queen to play in Argentina in 1981 was down to then president-in-waiting Viola and his political move to influence young people to vote. For him. He became president shortly after Queen's tour but only lasted until the end of that year before being ousted. The Argentinian and Brazilian audiences were fervid and excitable. In Mexico it was volatile and venal, the term corruption taken to a different level.

Queen did return to Brazil, finally playing Rio de Janeiro in January 1985, when they headlined the two Saturday nights of the enormous Rock in Rio festival. In the interim period, facilities and organisation had improved greatly and the two shows, on a vast stage, went very smoothly. Normally at Queen shows only the crew were allowed onstage, or very occasionally VIPs when the band's wives and special guests could watch from the wings for a short time. At Rio, due to the number of acts playing and the covering media, there were several people in the dark shadows of the wings, who were kept at bay by security. One figure edged closer to my area and leaned on my workbox flight case to get a better view of the show. I was on the edge of giving this middle-aged man some serious verbal, but when his hardened face became clearer I chose not to. It was escaped Great Train Robber, Ronnie Biggs, living in exile in Rio.

Previous page: An armed guard, one of many patrolling the stage, poses in front of John's equipment in São Paulo, Brazil.

Above: The band at afternoon soundcheck before their first South American show at Vélez Sarsfield stadium, Buenos Aires.

Opposite: John and me in the dressing room after the first momentous show, and a piano tuner working on Fred's Steinway D grand piano. Tuning was always a problem in the heat and humidity of South America, so the piano was also fine-tuned just before the show, and the setting taken for the guitar and bass strobe tuners. Guitars were also tuned just before the band took the stage. Below this is the view from Roger's drum kit during afternoon soundcheck and later, just prior to the show at Vélez Sarsfield, Buenos Aires, although the stadium clock shows the same time. The show started around midnight.

Above: Fred at soundcheck at Morumbi Stadium in São Paulo.

Below: A bonding football match between our Anglo-American team and the local Brazilian crew. Brian and his son came along to cheer for us. Alongside is Jim Beach, Queen's business manager and legal adviser, there to ensure fair play.

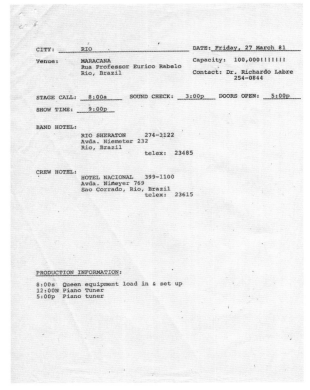

CITY: RIO   DATE: Friday, 27 March 81

Venue: MARACANA   Capacity: 100,000!!!!!!!
              Rua Professor Eurico Rabelo
              Rio, Brazil   Contact: Dr. Richardo Labre
                                         254-0844

STAGE CALL: 8:00a   SOUND CHECK: 3:00p   DOORS OPEN: 5:00p

SHOW TIME: 9:00p

BAND HOTEL:
              RIO SHERATON   274-1122
              Avda. Niemeter 232
              Rio, Brazil
                          telex: 23485

CREW HOTEL:
              HOTEL NACIONAL   399-1100
              Avda. Nimeyer 769
              Sao Corrado, Rio, Brazil
                          telex: 23615

PRODUCTION INFORMATION:

8:00a Queen equipment load in & set up
12:00N Piano Tuner
5:00p Piano tuner

Opposite, clockwise from top left: 'You are here!' The Production manager points to São Paulo on a map of Brazil on a tour T shirt during loading of our chartered 747 cargo plane after the shows; a tour itinerary page for the show that didn't happen in the Maracana, the hallowed playing surface of the national stadium deemed suitable for only football, Frank Sinatra and the Pope; Morumbi Stadium in São Paulo.

Above: Brian and Freddie perform 'Love Of My Life'. It was an emotional part of the show with audience singalong. And quite overwhelming.

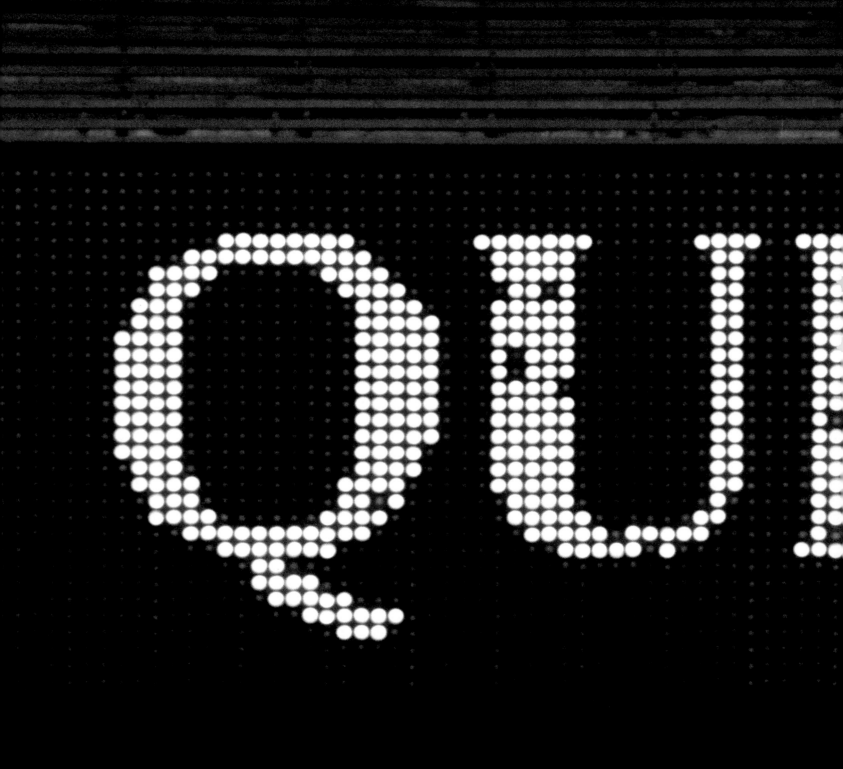

GLS PRODUCTIONS INC.

1509 Crossroads Of The World, Suite 104, Hollywood, California 90028 (213) 462-7101 Telex: GLS LSA 18-1384

QUEEN IN CARACAS

BAND PARTY

Freddie Mercury	(Alfred Mason)	1 bedroom suite
Roger Taylor	(Roy Tanner)	1 bedroom suite
John Deacon	(Jason Dane)	1 bedroom suite
Brian May	(Chris Mullins)	1 bedroom suite
Paul Prenter		single
Malcolm Ross		single
Jim Beach		single
Peter Freestone		single
Wally Verson		single
Wally Gore		single
David Kamppila		single
Neal Preston		single

GERRY STICKELLS, President   CHRIS LAMB, Vice-President

Edificio Anauco
Sótano Uno
PARQUE CENTRAL
Tlf.-5737013
CARACAS
Fosforos de Regalo P.V.P. sin valor comercial

Caracas, Venezuela. Above is a room list from the tour itinerary, showing the band and their entourage of personal assistants, management, security, wardrobe and tour photographer Neal Preston. The band have aliases, to avoid unwanted attention and phone calls.

Mexico offered the worst working conditions we ever encountered.

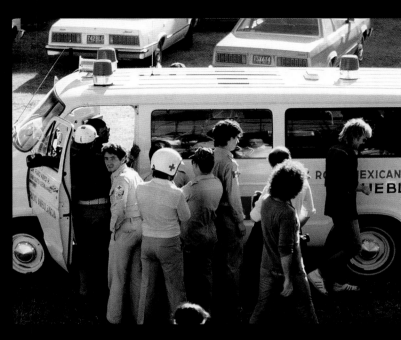

Left: Puebla Stadium, Mexico, shortly after the crowd had broken down the gates to the stadium and flooded in.

Above: Roger exiting an ambulance that had been used for the band to gain access to the stadium unnoticed. It was mayhem outside.

ROCK IN RIO

FESTIVAL

JANEIRO/85

Muita agitação no Galeão à chegada do Queen. O baterista Roger Taylor (cabelo louro, curto, de óculos escuros) observa o entusiasmo de uma fã, enquanto bem mais tranqüilo, carregando a própria bagagem, John Deacon, o baixista, consegue passar pela multidão

O som do Rock teve ontem o sim de Elba Ramalho, Herbert Viana e Lulu Santos. Também ontem chegaram três dos quatro membros do Queen, entre eles John Deacon (C), baixista. Hoje vem Freddie Mercury (Pág. 7, Caderno B e editorial Rock in Rio)

ROCK IN RIO

Queen topped the bill at this multi-band festival, playing shows on successive weekends. It was their biggest ever audience, estimated at up to 300,000 per show, but I doubt if anybody knows the real figures.

Newspaper cuttings show the front page of the biggest paper in Rio, *Jornal Do Brasil*. John 'Collie' Collins and I are reported as being John Deacon and Roger Taylor arriving at Rio Airport! As we carry our own bags and load them into a Volkswagen van...

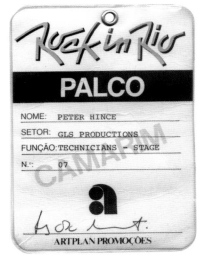

CHAPTER 7
VIDEOS

Queen's video for 'Bohemian Rhapsody' is considered the birth of the 'pop promo'. A seminal piece of moving imagery that generated a whole sub-industry in the music business.

There had been many promotional films and clips by bands before, notably The Beatles and The Stones, but not on the visual scale and grandeur of 'Bo Rhap'.

Produced at a cost of just a few thousand pounds during rehearsals at Elstree film studios for Queen's upcoming UK Night At The Opera tour, it only took three or four run-throughs of the live footage before the band stood on beer crates with black drapes around them to achieve photographer Mick Rock's classic cover image from the *Queen II* album.

The impact was enormous and complimented the epic song perfectly. Moreover, it was particularly useful in that it could be played on *Top of The Pops* and other TV shows while the band were away touring and unable to drop into the BBC Television Centre to mime to an audience of gawping, spotty, badly-dancing youths.

It's fair to say that Queen videos were hit and miss. 'Bo Rhap' a definite hit. The follow up for 'You're My Best Friend' by the same director, Bruce Gowers, a miss. It was shot during rehearsals at Ridge Farm for the album *A Day At The Races*, in the midst of the record-breaking hot summer of 1976. So the idea of filling an un-air-conditioned barn with hundreds of lit candles was perhaps not the greatest, but then creative types are not always practically minded. It became unbearable, with people coughing on the smoke in the confined space and on the edge of passing out from the heat as they spilled out into the daylight.

Video shoots, although seemingly exciting to the outsider, are actually long, drawn-out days of hanging around between takes, as lighting, camera changes and directorial decisions are made.

The tedium of waiting on a chilly set for union tea and meal breaks as countless polystyrene cups of tea and coffee – and, as the day drew on, vodka – are consumed.

Videos became a chore that needed to be done, and somewhat of an inconvenience, especially for the road crew. Hence Queen doing several 'live' performance videos: 'Fat Bottomed Girls', filmed during rehearsals in Dallas, 'Don't Stop Me Now' recorded between shows at the Forest National in Brussels – the same venue provided the backdrop for live and mimed footage for 'Hammer to Fall' in 1984 – and not forgetting the performance for 'Another One Bites The Dust', squeezed in during a soundcheck in Detroit!

What follows is a selection of images from just some of the video shoots I attended during my time with Queen. In 1981, MTV was born and the bar was raised. A band's visual output became far more important than it had been previously. It was not until late 1983, however, that the band began to do epic productions costing a small fortune to promote their singles.

Earlier shoots included the videos for 'Somebody To Love', 'We Will Rock You', 'Crazy Little Thing Called Love' and 'Play The Game' – which is where I shot the image of Fred jumping off the drum kit, used for the cover for the single 'Another One Bites The Dust' and in countless other forms of promotion all over the world. This video is the first to feature Fred with a moustache.

In 1982, the 'Back Chat' and 'Calling All Girls' videos, both from the *Hot Space* album, were shot in the same studio in Wandsworth, back to back.

After the somewhat limited success of *Hot Space*, Queen had left Elektra records in the US and Canada, Japan and Australasia and

signed a worldwide deal with EMI and its associate labels. The feeling was positive and the follow-up album, *The Works*, gave Queen the opportunity to 'give it the works'! The band rallied and made what most feel was a proper 'Queen album' with power ballads and anthemic songs that live audiences could join in singing, as well as heavy rock and well-crafted rock and pop songs.

'Radio Ga Ga', penned by Roger Taylor, was the first single. The video was shot at Carlton Television studios, with the main scenes on a vast sound stage in Shepperton Studios just outside London, while recording for *The Works* album continued in Munich. Director David Mallet, who had compiled and edited the stock footage video for 'Under Pressure', was brought in. David had also directed *The Kenny Everett Television Show*, fronted by a close friend and big supporter of Queen.

Using vintage footage from director Fritz Lang's *Metropolis*, 'Radio Ga Ga' took the band back to making big, bold statements with their videos – whatever the cost. Freddie was always the one pushing to go bigger and better when these issues were discussed.

Using members of the band's fan club, the memorable hand-clapping scenes transcended into the live shows and most notably at Live Aid – where even non-Queen fans clapped along in time.

The follow-up single was John Deacon's 'I Want To Break Free'. Once again, an epic video for the MTV generation was planned. This time, Queen would dress up in drag as a comic homage to English soap operas, an idea first mooted by Roger Taylor's long-term partner, Dominique. Perhaps surprisingly, all the band were quickly on board with the idea.

The resultant video was a big hit, as was the single – but not in America. MTV had banned the video and Queen's US record company asked the band for a different one, a performance on a mocked-up stage or similar. The band refused and, consequently, an already-tense situation became escalated.

Queen already held the record for being the first band to have a video banned by MTV, for the 1982 single 'Body Language', as it was deemed too 'steamy' (i.e. erotic). Paradoxically, it became a reasonable hit in the US, whereas 'Break Free' failed to make the top 50.

Americans, it seems, simply did not 'get' the 'Break Free' video. It was fun, a pastiche, men dressing as women in the old tradition of comedy and music hall. The irony is that America loved Monty Python, who regularly dressed in drag, so it's seemingly okay for comedians to do it – just not rock stars.

It's a real shame that this incident sparked the beginning of the end for Queen's huge popularity in the USA. For *The Works* album PR, they simply made a quick trip to New York and conducted a few selected interviews. The subsequent Works tour did not include the USA, for the first time since they'd made it big. I thought at the time that America was a fickle mistress and needed wooing and cajoling.

I recall Fred saying something along the lines of, 'Oh, don't worry, when we're ready we'll go back and play a few of the big places.' And though tour manager Gerry Stickells did have some dates optioned in the USA, it never happened.

Behind the scenes at the video for 'Somebody To Love', shot at Wessex
studios in Highbury, London, during the recording of *A Day At The Races*.

Shot in the snowy, freezing cold garden of Roger's country house in Surrey
– before he had actually moved in – this is the video for 'We Will Rock You'.
Video cameras were huge and even supposedly portable roving cameras
had to be tethered by thick cables to power supplies or operators wearing
huge backpacks.

Shot in 1979 at Trillion studios in Soho, London, the promotional video for 'Crazy Little Thing Called Love' saw Fred's image shift a little more towards the 'leather biker' look. This was a fun video to be not only present at, but a part of, the road crew's handclaps appearing through holes in the catwalk.

The 'Play The Game' shoot is where I shot the well-known photograph of Fred jumping off the drum kit (overleaf). I could see in advance that I only had maybe four attempts to catch Fred in mid-air, as the Hasselblad square format camera would only allow me one frame per jump, as it had to be hand-cranked to wind on to the next frame. The other frames show where it didn't quite work, or his jump wasn't quite as good. A cross-screen filter was added to the lens to give the starburst effect for the studio lights.

Scenes from the 'Back Chat' and 'Calling All Girls' videos, which were filmed back-to-back in a London studio.

"In 1981, MTV was born and the bar was raised. A band's visual output became far more important than it had been previously."

'Radio Ga Ga' had been hugely successful in the charts, with
the exception of America where it had been moderately
received, although the video did receive an MTV Awards
nomination for best art direction.

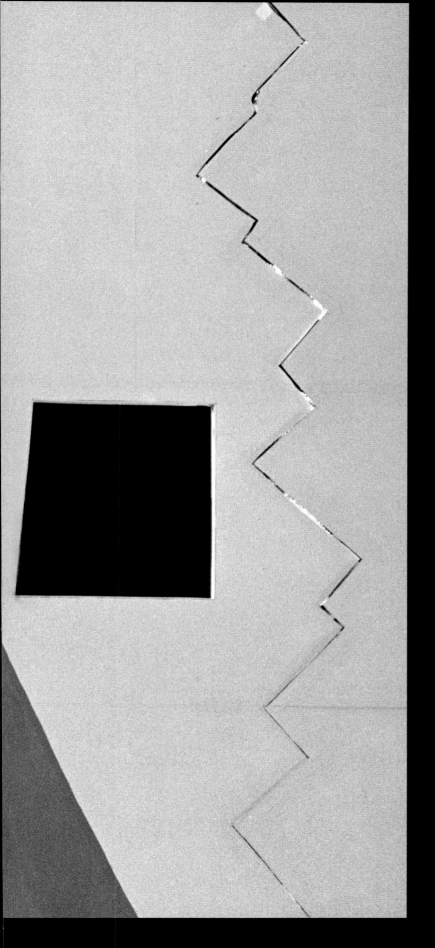

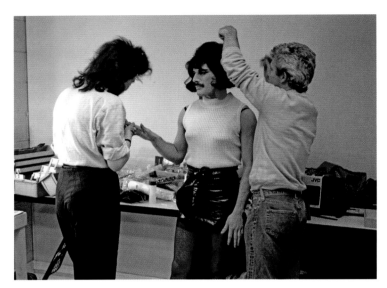

Scenes from production of the band's controversial
– at least in the US – video for 'I Want To Break Free'.

The scenes featuring miners were filmed at Limehouse Studios in London's Docklands, with the 'dressing up' shots recorded the following day on a set built in Battersea Studios.

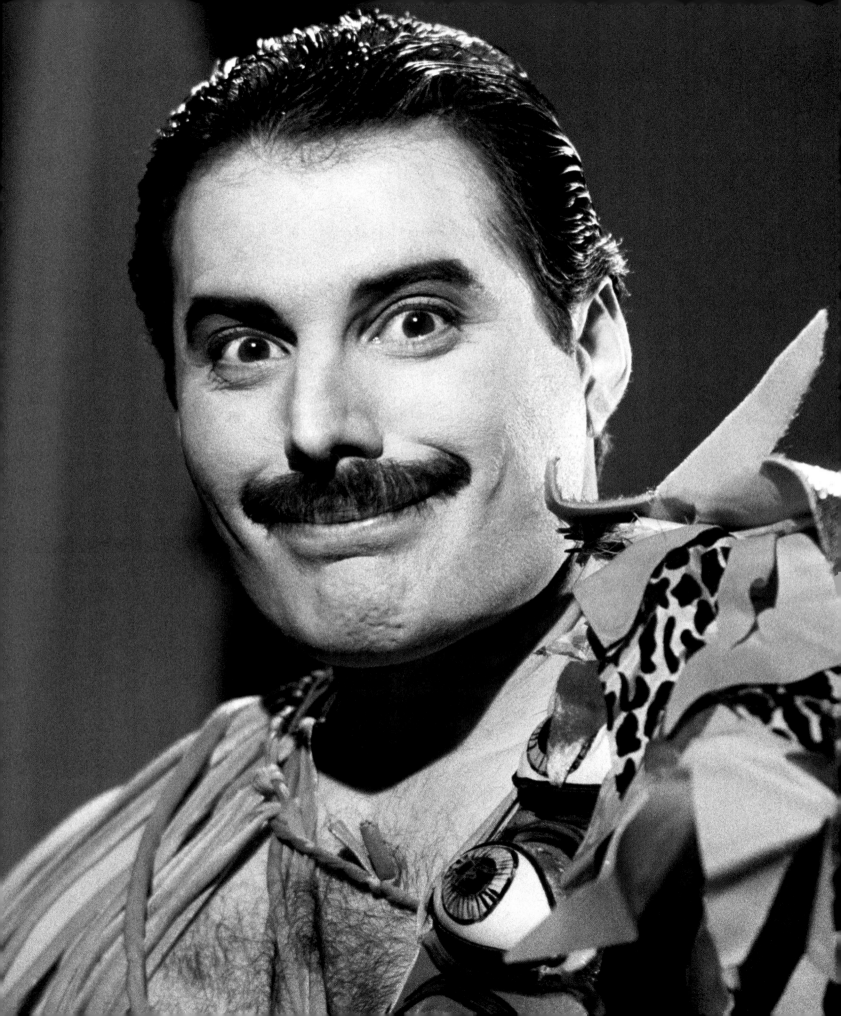

Is it Fred or Salvador Dalí? With his upturned moustache and surreal outfit Fred does do a fair imitation, although no doubt it was unintentional.

He is not often portrayed smiling or laughing, but he would quite comfortably do that for me. We had a good relationship and rapport, built up over a long time, which I think went a long way to getting images of Freddie Mercury that other photographers couldn't. This was taken on the set of the video for 'It's A Hard Life' in Arri Studios, Munich, in 1984.

CHAPTER 8

LIVE AID
AND BEYOND

We all have days in our lives that are monumental, filled with joy, excitement, a sense of achievement.

A wedding (or final decree of divorce...) day, the birth of a child, success in sport or our chosen career. I've been lucky to have had many special days in my life, and Saturday July 13th 1985 at Wembley Stadium was certainly one of the biggest and most memorable. Live Aid.

However, it's only in retrospect that I realise the enormity of the day; at the time it was all about doing my job and praying nothing technical went wrong in front of a worldwide audience of almost two billion people. No pressure then!

Queen had initially declined the invitation to play Live Aid. They had not been asked to join the cast of superstars to record the Band Aid single 'Do They Know It's Christmas?' and rumours were circulating that it was a result of the adverse publicity brought about by Queen playing Sun City in apartheid-era South Africa shortly before.

At this point in their career Queen were at a crossroads and I believe there was a real chance of them breaking up or at least taking a break to pursue other individual projects.

They had been together for around fifteen years and continually toured and recorded; their work ethic was relentless. *The Works* album and tour had been very successful, but they no longer had the popularity in America they had worked so hard to achieve. They were tired, maybe somewhat jaded and the spontaneity of ideas and desire to keep moving forward wasn't evident. Moreover, the band were human beings with families and lives outside of Queen.

Bob Geldof knew what he wanted for Live Aid at Wembley. The biggest bands, who would make an impact. He attempted to woo Fred at September restaurant on Fulham Road, but Fred politely declined, saying they were not a political band. Geldof persisted, saying this was not a political event, it was about saving lives. Which, in a sense, does become political.

Once everyone in Queen had agreed to take part they approached the event, as aways, with total professionalism. Tour manager Gerry Stickells and their sound and monitor engineers were flown in to London from America, as rehearsals were booked at the Shaw Theatre on Euston Road. In fact, it had not been very long since the band had played together, The Works album tour having finished with an Australia, New Zealand and Japan leg fewer than two months previously.

Queen were renowned for putting on exciting live shows, with huge lighting rigs, smoke, and pyrotechnics, an event full of energy and dynamism. 'Blind 'em and deafen 'em!' But Live Aid would be different: every band had the same level playing field, no sound check, no special effects, go on, play your 20-minute set, get off.

Queen focused and honed their set to perfection, playing some of their biggest hits that had already been proven to work live, in outdoor stadiums around the world. The choice of the final six songs came together quite quickly, which was somewhat of a surprise, as the band could often argue and debate for ages when making collective decisions. It did not include any of John Deacon's songs – a little strange, bearing in mind he'd written their biggest ever single in America and many other hits. But John rarely made a fuss, he went with the flow. I bought some big, white plastic clocks and put them at the front of the stage, so as the band ran through the proposed sets they could monitor how long each one took and what time was left.

On the day of Live Aid the schedule was run like clockwork. We arrived at our allotted time and unloaded the truck, putting Queen's equipment into a holding area. Then, on cue, began setting up the stage – off-stage. The Live Aid stage was circular and divided into 3 sections, like a slice of pie, 120 degrees in mathematical terms. While one act was playing, another was setting up and the previous act were breaking down their equipment. It was hectic and the pressure was on everybody involved. Queen had a lot of equipment with very precise settings and positioning. However, the Queen stage crew of just three were highly experienced and knew exactly how to make this stage feel just like any other stage for Queen, a home from home. But the tight time limit was a real challenge; as Queen were being introduced and bouncing onstage to acknowledge the audience, I was still tuning John's bass guitar.

I don't recall much being said before their performance, and if Queen were nervous they certainly didn't show it. Just the usual courtesies exchanged in the dressing room from the crew, and confirmation that all was fine.

Once the band had settled and Fred began 'Bo Rhap' at the piano, there was a sigh of relief that all was okay, despite everything having been checked and doubled-checked. When Fred grabbed his 'wand' microphone and took to centre stage with a real swagger to begin 'Radio Ga Ga' you could sense the energy building. When the entire stadium raised their arms for the now-famous handclaps you knew Queen had the audience firmly on their side. Despite the script of a 20-minute (or thereabouts) set, Fred was spontaneous, he danced with onstage cameramen then gave his legendary call-and-response vocal phrases with the audience. Now it was at a different level. This was not a Queen audience, but they responded as if they were, and by the end of 'We Are The Champions' it was clear Queen had won, a resounding cup final performance at the national stadium. No extra time or penalties required.

Why were Queen so good at Live Aid? There are many discussions, articles and debates, but at the end of the day they were a tight band who could really play. Four exceptional musicians who raised the bar that day, fuelled by a remarkable front man. And they were louder...

During this historical performance I was somewhat immune to the response as I focused on Fred and John and getting all my cues and handovers spot on. No doubt once the truck doors were closed and we all relaxed, there was a feeling of both relief and elation. But it's only in hindsight that I and others fully appreciate what Queen achieved that day.

It not only gave the band belief again that they still had something to offer as a unit, but showed the world and non-Queen fans just how good they were. This was at a time when they were not especially popular with the media.

Live Aid was an adrenaline boost, affirmation for Queen that they should carry on, which they did shortly afterwards, recording the *Highlander* movie soundtrack and *A Kind of Magic* album. Suddenly, Queen were the band everybody wanted to see and a year later in 1986 were back at Wembley as part of their final Magic tour.

WEMBLEY STADIUM

Harvey Goldsmith, Maurice Jones & Bob Geldof
present for

BAND AID

LIVE AID

(See Press for details)

SAT., 13 JULY, 1985

GATES OPEN 10.00 a.m.

No ticket genuine unless it carries the
Wembley Lion superimposed on the Towers

Ticket £5 incl. VAT plus **£20 donation**

All proceeds to BAND AID

TURNSTILES

D

5441

TO BE RETAINED

ISSUED SUBJECT TO THE
CONDITIONS ON BACK

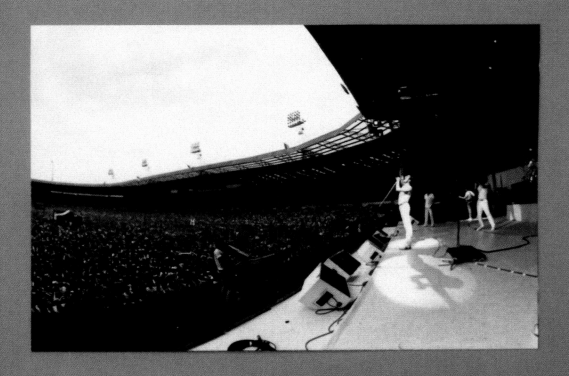

LIVE AID

July 13, 1985
Presented to
PETER HINCE
Thank you from
Brian, Freddie, John & Roger

QUEEN

Mr Farenheit.

Above: Brian, London, 1986.

Opposite: Fred on set with actress Debbie Ash.
He looks like a 1940s Hollywood matinee idol.

LOVE IS THE HERO

Shortly before the Magic tour, I was helping out Billy Squier, who was recording in London. Billy had known Queen for many years. After the huge success of *The Game* album, producer Mack was hired to work on Billy's *Don't Say No* album, which became an enormous hit in the USA, though had limited success in other territories. The follow-up album, again produced by Mack, featured vocals by Freddie, Brian and Roger, and again was a big hit; in fact outselling Queen's *Hot Space* album at the time.

Billy chose to support Queen on the 1982 Hot Space tour, when he could have filled arenas on his own. But Billy was honoured to be on tour with Queen and held huge admiration for them.

He was finishing his latest album, *Enough is Enough* at Sarm Studios in East London, where Queen had spent many months of their career working on their early albums up to *News of The World* in 1977. Billy spent some time socially with Freddie, as Fred was keen to show him his new home, Garden Lodge, which had finally been refurbished. Billy played Fred a few songs during late nights and early mornings, and Fred enthused about them. Being Fred, he made suggestions, which Billy was delighted with. Within a day or two Fred was back at Sarm and reworked two of Billy's songs. 'Heart of Mine' became 'Lady With a Tenor Sax' – Fred was already excitedly directing the potential video with 'lots of hot girls swaying with saxes'. He then put a piano introduction and vocals onto 'Love is The Hero' – a title he loved, claiming it was the perfect title for a song.

This was an example of Freddie's generosity. He would often help out people and never ask for any reward or credit. I know Billy is so proud of the two songs they worked on and I personally agree that 'Love is The Hero' is a great title – and a great song.

FREDDIE AND FREDDIE

After a show in Madrid, I was summoned to the dressing room – and told to bring my camera. It was at Fred's instruction, so the other crew covered for me as I did as I was asked. Fred wanted a photograph of him with the promoter's dog, also called Freddie, as you can see on his backstage pass! I quickly shot off half a roll of film and the joy in Fred as he cuddles the dog is so nice to see. He is often seen with his beloved cats, but I don't know if there is another image of him holding a dog.

It's interesting that Freddie is associated so closely with the yellow jacket and white trousers outfit from that tour – every tribute singer seems to choose it. Freddie had countless different looks and costumes through his career, yet this final tour choice is what people who never saw Queen associate him with – that and a moustache.

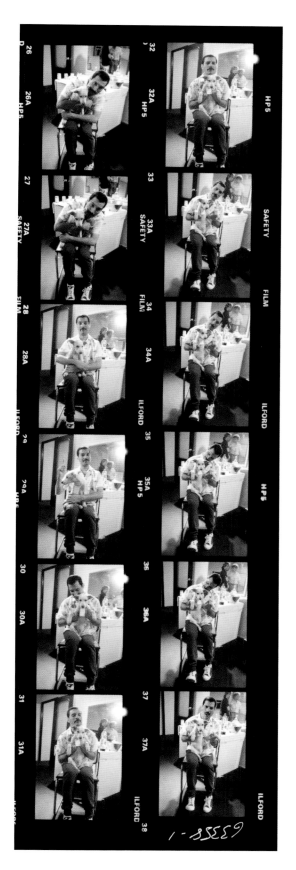

HIS MAJESTY

In early 1987 I received a call in my studio from Freddie, saying that he wanted to come over in the evening and do a 'fun shot'. And could I arrange everything? Which meant of course, 'Get it sorted, I'll be over.' Fred was somebody you couldn't really say no to. He wanted a studio image of the crown and robes he had worn on stage for the final encore on the Magic tour the previous year.

  He liked the contrast of the grand and the prosaic, the opulent costume and regal pose alongside the everyday studio backdrop of metal poles and paper backgrounds – which is why I didn't crop those elements from the edges of the shot. It was an act, Fred was a performer who needed the back-up systems and props to create the illusion that was Freddie Mercury.

THE GREAT PRETENDER

This was a shoot for the life-size cut-out figures of Fred to be used in his 'Great Pretender' video. A black and white Polaroid was taken using a special back that would fit onto a Hasselblad camera. It gave an exact 6×6cm image (the same format as the film that would be used) to check for lighting, composition and importantly to show Fred how it looked. With this type of B&W Polaroid there was a negative which, when you peeled the backing paper away to reveal the positive image, could be wiped clean, saved and, if required, printed from. This particular negative had some kind of chemical contamination giving the effect of stars over Fred's image. He really liked it. But we'd already shot the cover for 'The Great Pretender' single a few months previously – otherwise I think Fred would have considered this image.

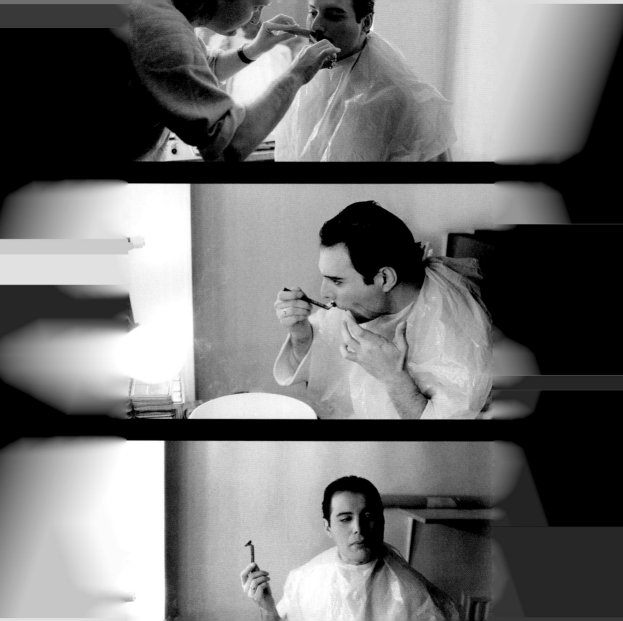

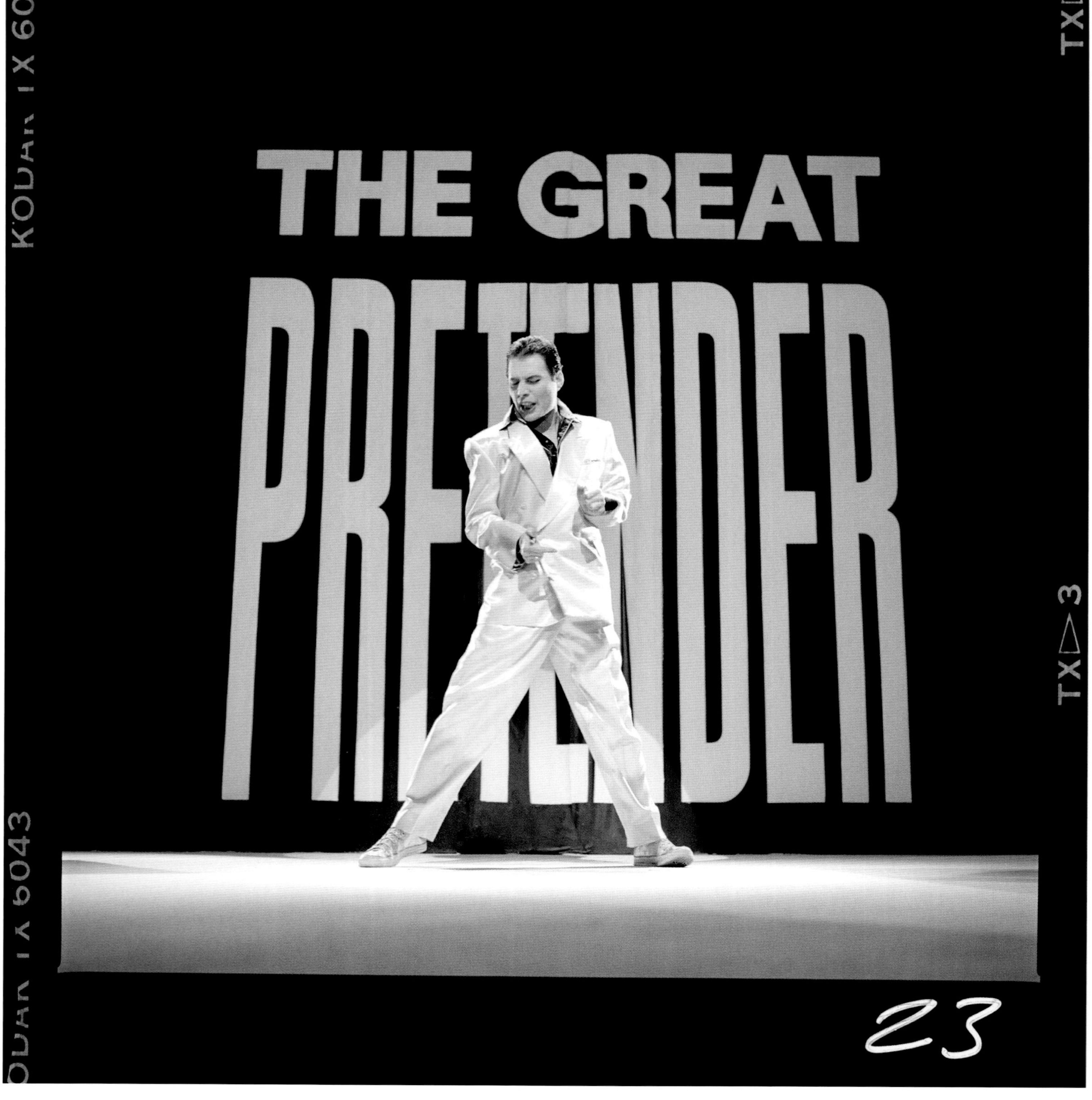
THE GREAT
PRETENDER
23

Above: Mike Moran – musician, composer, arranger and producer, who co-wrote 'Barcelona' with Freddie. Portrait taken in my London studio. Below left he appears on set, as a conductor for the 'Barcelona' video.

MAJOR DEACON

In 1988, John Deacon guested in a video for the single 'This is The Chorus' by comedy band Morris Minor and The Majors. John, along with the band, is dressed as a Rick Astley lookalike on the single cover, which I shot in my studio. The band were managed by Pete Brown, who started an agency for producing and managing comedy acts after he left Queen's management in 1979.

Harvey Goldsmith proudly presents

QUEEN

Status Quo

BIG COUNTRY

BELOUIS SOME

H

HOSPITALITY

SATURDAY 9th AUGUST 1986
KNEBWORTH PARK

NO BACKSTAGE
ACCESS

NOT TRANSFERABLE MUST BE STUCK ON

I can't explain why, but at the final ever Queen show at Knebworth in August 1986, I just somehow felt it would be the last. And it was.

Freddie always maintained he would never become a parody of himself, puffing and panting to get around the stage in ridiculous outfits when his figure was not as lithe as it once was. If he couldn't give his all then he would bow out gracefully. Which he did.

People ask me what would Fred have been doing if he was still alive? I answer that it would have been whatever he wanted to do, but definitely involving music. No doubt he would have continued with Queen projects, or more collaborations perhaps? Writing film scores or maybe a solo album of classics in a different style, just him and a piano? He could have gone back to his art and painted or designed?

Whatever he did it had to excite and intrigue him. Freddie always surprised people and I've no doubt he would have continued to do that.

Published in 2023 by Welbeck

An Imprint of Welbeck Non-Fiction Limited,

part of Welbeck Publishing Group.

Offices in London: 20 Mortimer Street, London W1T 3JW &

Sydney: Level 17, 207 Kent St, Sydney NSW 2000 Australia.

www.welbeckpublishing.com

Photographs © 2023 Peter Hince

Text © 2023 Peter Hince

Design © 2023 Welbeck Non-fiction Limited

A CIP catalogue record for this book is available from the British Library

ISBN 978 1 80279 627 8

Associate Publisher: Joe Cottington

Design: Russell Knowles

Production: Rachel Burgess

Printed in China

10 9 8 7 6 5 4 3 2 1

ACKNOWLEDGEMENTS

My sincere thanks and appreciation go to Queen – Freddie, John, Brian and Roger and the many people I met and worked with during my rock 'n' roll years. These include (in no particular order) Mary Austin, Veronica Deacon, Chrissy May, Dominique Taylor, Joe Fanelli, Jim Hutton, Gerry and Sylvia Stickells, Reinhold and Ingrid Mack, Fred Mandel, Billy Squier, Mike Moran, Morgan Fisher, Jimmy Barnett, Joe Trovato, Richie Anderson, Phil John, Mott The Hoople, David Bowie, Mick & Suzi Ronson, Robin Mayhew, Mick Hince, Chris Taylor, Brian Zellis, John Collins, Edwin Shirley, Chris Wright & Ian Haynes at Rock-It Cargo, Jim Devenney, Trip Khalaf, Mike Stone, Geoff Workman, Roy Thomas-Baker, John Harris, Brian Spencer, Tony Williams, Dane Clark, Neal Preston, Peter Lubin, Mike Wilderink, Pete Brown, David Wigg, Pete Cornish, Dick Ollet, Vicky Everett.

In the production of this photo book, I am grateful to the following for their support, input and enthusiasm: Karin Braun, Carrie Kania at Iconic Images, Joe Cottington, Russell Knowles and all at Welbeck Publishing, John Cleur, Tony Window and all at Metro Imaging, Stephen Hoffman of Galerie Stephen Hoffman, Chris Close, Julianna Mitchell, Vernon Reeves, Klaus Kalde, Alastair Campbell, Mark Blake, Niccolo Chimenti, Stefano Pesenti.

And all those others who pestered, encouraged and cajoled me into producing this photo book.

Dedicated to my parents, who still wonder when I'll get a proper job...

www.peterhince.co.uk

Dear Ratty —

Wishing you a
Merry Christmas
and a
Happy New Year
from the
Preening, Pouting, Posing,
Posturing Old Tart

lots of love —

Freddie